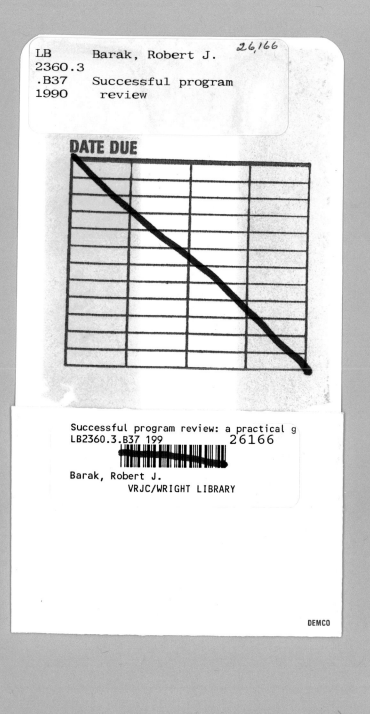

SUCCESSFUL PROGRAM REVIEW

❋❋❋❋❋

A Practical Guide
to Evaluating Programs
in Academic Settings

Robert J. Barak
Barbara E. Breier

SUCCESSFUL PROGRAM REVIEW

*A Practical Guide
to Evaluating Programs
in Academic Settings*

Jossey-Bass Publishers

San Francisco • Oxford • 1990

SUCCESSFUL PROGRAM REVIEW
A Practical Guide to Evaluating Programs in Academic Settings
by Robert J. Barak and Barbara E. Breier

Copyright © 1990 by: Jossey-Bass Inc., Publishers
350 Sansome Street
San Francisco, California 94104

&

Jossey-Bass Limited
Headington Hill Hall
Oxford OX3 0BW

Library of Congress Cataloging-in-Publication Data

Barak, Robert J.
    Successful program review : a practical guide to evaluating
programs in academic settings / Robert J. Barak, Barbara E. Breier.
        p.   cm. — (The Jossey-Bass higher education series)
    Includes bibliographical references.
    ISBN 1-55542-241-1
    1. Universities and colleges—United States—Departments—
Evaluation.   2. Educational evaluation—United States.
3. Universities and colleges—United States—Accreditation.
I. Breier, Barbara E., date.   II. Title.   Series.
    LB2360.3.B37   1990
378.1'07--dc20   90-30450
                                                             CIP

Manufactured in the United States of America

The paper in this book meets the guidelines for
permanence and durability of the Committee on
Production Guidelines for Book Longevity of the
Council on Library Resources.

JACKET DESIGN BY WILLI BAUM

FIRST EDITION

Code 9044

The Jossey-Bass
Higher Education Series

Contents

Preface

Practically every college, regardless of its size or mission, engages in some form of program review. Indeed, a 1982 study commissioned by the National Center for Higher Education Management Systems revealed that 82 percent of colleges and universities and most higher education boards have some form of program review (Barak, 1982a). The process depends on the personalities and problems unique to each campus. Those responsible for developing, implementing, and evaluating a program review are faced with countless decisions and piles of data they must sort and evaluate in order to reach conclusions about the program's quality and effectiveness.

   The participants in a program review range from college administrators and staff to faculty, from governing bodies and state agencies to legislative committees. All these parties are involved in program review activities at different times. Some have direct responsibility for the process, while others are primarily concerned with the results. Regardless of their involvement, these parties need to know what the process involves, how the results are obtained, how they themselves are to be involved in the process, and what actions are expected of them. All too frequently program reviews are undertaken hastily with little planning and preparation, few resources to support the activity, and little knowledge of what the process entails. The resulting activities are frustrating to those involved, yield poor results, and undermine confidence in future program reviews.

Purpose of the Book

Successful Program Review is designed to help educators and administrators conduct a successful program review and overcome the pitfalls noted above. Based on the experiences we have gleaned from countless on-campus interviews, as well as our own experiences as administrators and process consultants, the book addresses the needs of both the inexperienced program reviewer and the seasoned veteran who would like to fine-tune and revise an existing process. There is no "true model" for all institutions. In fact, to avoid conveying any connotation of approval of particular processes, we have refrained from using the word *model*. Rather, we outline the essential steps of a successful program review and present ample alternatives so that readers can choose the approach that seems most appropriate for their institutions. This book is not intended as a reference for scholars who are conducting research in this field. Nor have we tried to provide detailed discussions of alternative approaches to evaluation or assessment. Detailed discussions of these subjects are available in other publications. We do, however, describe successful reviews based on our research, consulting, and experience.

While much has been written about program review in recent years, a good deal of the literature is anecdotal and based on limited research. Until now, no one has synthesized the various opinion pieces, personal experience, research, and theoretical work into a guide for practical use. This volume will fill that void.

The purpose of this book is to provide a step-by-step guide to the program review process. It is designed to give readers the practical advice they need to conduct a successful program review. The book outlines for the novice all the steps necessary to design, implement, and evaluate a program review; it also provides information to those with experience who are assessing their established processes. Program review is a dynamic process and as programs change, so does the process. If the program review process is not continually evaluated, it will quickly become obsolete. This volume also serves all of those who are asked to serve on review committees, evaluate reports, and make judgments related to program review activities. As we work as consultants and conduct research into the program review process, hundreds of educators have asked for practical advice regarding program reviews. This book is a direct response to their requests.

Background

In this book we draw extensively on the literature and on our research and combined experience in working with some 150 colleges and universities, numerous system and district offices, and 23 state boards.

Our research base draws on both published and unpublished work we have undertaken over the past decade and a half. The published studies include Barak and Berdahl (1978), Barak (1982a), Barak and Miller (1986), and Breier (1985, 1988). Several unpublished studies were undertaken specifically for this volume (Barak, 1984, 1986; Breier, 1986a, 1986b) and are reported here for the first time. The first study, conducted in 1986 (Breier, 1986a) involved in-depth case studies at five colleges and universities. The purpose of the study was to test several hypotheses regarding program review that had been reached initially in a study in Kansas (Breier, 1985). The five colleges, selected for their differences from the previous study, were William Jewell College, Texas Lutheran College, San Antonio College, Tulane University, and the University of Florida. Results of this study confirmed and expanded the previous study and are presented in Chapters Five and Six. The second unpublished study (Breier, 1986b) was conducted on the role of consultants in program reviews. A survey instrument was mailed to sixty consultants regarding their involvement and concerns associated with program reviews. The results of this study are covered in Chapter Three.

Overview of the Chapters

Successful Program Review is organized into chapters based on the key issues faced by those who want to learn how program review works, implement a program review, evaluate a program review procedure, or understand the specific roles of the people involved in a program review. Consequently, the book can be used in different ways depending on the reader's intent. Following Chapter One, the introductory chapter, three chapters address the preliminary, review, and postreview activities.

Chapter Two addresses preview activities. It explores the need to understand clearly at the outset the purposes and objectives of the review—to determine the audiences served, the resources needed, and the conceptualization and approval of the review plan. It also addresses the critical need to involve those affected by the review in the process as well as the need for ongoing communication.

Chapter Three covers the active phase of the review, including the need for continuing communications; the collection, review, and analysis of data; the use of consultants; the preparation of self-studies; and the coordination of all these activities. This is the stage at which the review itself takes place.

Chapter Four covers critical postreview activities. These normally include the preparation of reports and recommendations, the utilization of the review results, and the evaluation of the review process referred to here as a meta-review. Since meta-reviews are relatively new to the literature, we discuss their role and effectiveness in detail.

Chapters Five and Six consider the major figures who play active parts in a program review. These chapters, written from the perspective of those who have participated in the review process, provide the reader with not only essential information about the roles but also a feeling for what they are like according to the participants. Chapter Five discusses faculty and institutional support, detailing the four main types of faculty involvement, ways to manage time and resource constraints, and the two levels of institutional support. We also cover the role of the institutional research office, the data requirements of the various review approaches, and the context of the specialized reports related to program reviews.

Chapter Six considers the administrative, governing board, and legislative roles in program review activities. As well as describing the roles of the chief executive officer, the chief academic officer, deans, and directors, we consider administrative involvement, the involvement of the governing boards or trustees, and the role of legislators and the governor's office. Their involvement has increased dramatically in recent years, and many of those serving in these positions are unfamiliar with program review activities. The chapter discusses the amount of time involved in the different approaches, the interpretation of data, the questions that board members or legislators should ask, and what kind of staff support is available.

Chapter Seven, the concluding chapter, describes how program review relates to accreditation, assessment, and planning. Program review occurs on campuses in conjunction with numerous other activities. This chapter explains how the program review is shaped by accreditation and assessment efforts and how the results of the program review can be incorporated into the strategic planning process and the other management activities on campus. Since program review does not occur in a vacuum, participants in the process must be aware of the dynamics at work on every college campus. The chapter concludes by reviewing the principles of the successful program review and offering some important lessons on institutionalizing the process.

It is our hope that this volume will prove a practical guide for anyone involved in program review. It is intended not to present models but to present processes that have been demonstrated as the most successful review techniques. As administrators continue to implement program review on college campuses, the process will continue to be modified and improved. We welcome all comments and suggestions from our readers.

Acknowledgments

We wish to acknowledge the assistance of Joy Cron, whose typing and editorial assistance were vital in the preparation of this book. We especially want to acknowledge the patience, help, and support of our families, without which the book would not have been completed on time. We also wish to thank the many colleges and universities, too numerous to mention here, whose experiences have enlightened this work. Grateful appreciation is expressed to colleagues and friends who have reviewed text, opened doors, and shown support in countless ways.

February 1990
Robert J. Barak
Des Moines, Iowa

Barbara E. Breier
Abilene, Texas

The Authors

❋❋❋❋❋

Robert J. Barak is deputy executive director and director of academic affairs and research for the Iowa Board of Regents. He received his B.S. degree (1967) from Michigan State University in divisional science, his M.A. degree (1971) from the University of Missouri in higher education, and his Ph.D. degree (1976) from the State University of New York, Buffalo, in higher education. He also has completed postdoctoral work at Harvard University. Barak has researched and written numerous books, articles, and papers on program review, including *Program Review in Higher Education* (1982) and *State-Level Academic Program Review for Higher Education* (1978, with R. Berdahl). He has served as consultant to more than 150 colleges and universities, 23 state agencies, and several regional higher education compacts, foundations, and higher education organizations, both nationally and internationally.

Barbara E. Breier is assistant to the provost and director of continuing education and evening programs at Hardin-Simmons University. She received her B.A. degree (1969) from Texas Christian University in English and history, her M.A. degree (1972) from Texas A&I University in English, and her

Ph.D. degree (1985) from the University of Kansas in higher education. Breier's main research activities have been in policy studies, educational evaluation, and related theories of organizational behavior. Her institutional experience with program review and evaluation spans six institutions over a nineteen-year career in higher education. She has served in various administrative and faculty positions at El Reno Junior College, Cameron University, the University of Kansas, William Jewell College, and Hardin-Simmons University. Author or coauthor of several articles on program review (covering program review in private colleges, internal versus external program review models, and mandated program review and program discontinuance), she has conducted extensive on-campus research in the program review process. Breier has served as consultant to both colleges and secondary schools on program review and planning and is currently conducting a funded research project on the role of denominational colleges in the twenty-first century.

SUCCESSFUL PROGRAM REVIEW

❋❋❋❋❋❋

*A Practical Guide
to Evaluating Programs
in Academic Settings*

1

Objectives and Principles
of Successful Program Review

Educational evaluation is not new but can be traced to antiquity (Kitto, 1969). What *is* new is the systematic and periodic application of modern evaluative techniques to educational programs. Starting in the late 1950s and early 1960s, various trends, primarily outside of higher education (for example, dissatisfaction with public school education, the influence of increased federal funds for education, the increase in vocational programs), resulted in pressure for greater effectiveness of educational programs (Popham, 1975). This pressure, in turn, led to the development and refinement of evaluation efforts primarily at the elementary and secondary levels. In the last two decades, similar pressures, often referred to as the "accountability movement," began to have an impact on higher education as well. Responding to these pressures, many colleges, universities, systems, and state-level boards began to adopt a specialized form of evaluation known as *program review* (Conrad and Wilson, 1985; Barak, 1986). The term no doubt arose from the fact that in most instances the focus of this evaluation was on academic programs, usually defined as a sequence of educational experiences leading to a degree or certificate. Today more than 82 percent of colleges and universities and most higher education boards have a

1

formal program review process (Barak, 1982a). It is for this reason that we focus this volume on developing new review processes and evaluating existing ones.

Program review, as used in this volume, is a type of evaluation aimed primarily at academic and instructional programs in colleges and universities. It differs from the traditional accreditation review of programs because it seeks to evaluate all programs, or a selected group of programs such as a graduate school, against a standard set of criteria. By using a standard set of criteria, faculty and administrators make judgments about a program's effectiveness. While some have condemned program reviews because of their personal experience with reviews that were poorly designed and executed, program reviews are neither good nor bad. They are a widely accepted tool in postsecondary education for assessing such characteristics as cost of program per student, effectiveness of faculty, and use of resources. Properly designed and executed, the program review can become a valuable tool for improving the quality, efficiency, and effectiveness of postsecondary education.

The earliest reviews in higher education were limited in the sense that they rarely covered all programs and were not systematic. At the university level (and even in some state-level reviews), the primary focus was on graduate education. At the two-year-college level, the focus was primarily on vocational education in response to federal requirements. Recently reviews are becoming more comprehensive, covering all academic programs at all levels.

The term *program review* includes many different evaluation techniques. Reviews are conducted at various levels (program, department, school, college, institution, system/district, and statewide) for many different purposes (ranging from improvement to termination) and involve a variety of figures (faculty, administrators, students, alumni, trustees, state board members, and staff as well as others).

Due to the many misconceptions regarding program review, we believe that any handbook on the subject should begin by defining key concepts and addressing issues critical to an understanding of program review. For the purposes of this volume, reviews can be thought of as ranging from *self-reviews* conducted by the faculty for the primary purpose of program improvement to *external reviews* conducted primarily for accountability purposes. In between these two extremes are reviews conducted for various purposes by a variety of persons. While it is possible to combine these two extremes in a single review, it is difficult to do so effectively. For this reason, we refer in this volume to program reviews as being either self-reviews (formative reviews) or external reviews (summative reviews).

Types of Reviews

At the risk of oversimplification, one can classify reviews into four basic types according to their primary motivation:

1. Formative reviews to improve the program
2. Summative reviews to aid selection, certification, or accountability
3. Public relations reviews to increase awareness or to sell a program's importance
4. Authoritative reviews to exercise authority

In a formative review the primary responsibility typically rests with the faculty connected with the program. Its main objective is to find ways to improve the program. Formative reviews are also conducted by departments, schools and colleges, and institutions. System/district and state-level reviews are seldom conducted primarily for the sole purpose of program improvement.

Summative reviews are rarely conducted by the faculty from the program under review. Generally they are conducted by departments, schools or districts, institutions, systems, and the state.

Public relations reviews are conducted rarely but have been known to occur at all levels from program to state. While not necessarily a whitewash, they do tend to be self-serving and are generally not regarded by professional evaluators as true evaluations. Responsibility for this type of review generally rests with those closest to the program, department, school or college, or system. The involvement of others is limited to the extent that they can contribute to the promotional purposes of the review.

Authoritative reviews are conducted by leaders primarily as an expression of their power, and may or may not be true evaluations. Several years ago, the head of one state's higher education agency confided to us that the primary purpose of certain review efforts was to demonstrate the agency's power. They may, incidentally, be useful for formative or, more frequently, summative purposes. This book will focus only on the summative and formative reviews because these are the most common types, the most legitimate forms of program evaluation, and those closest to our research and experience.

Another way to define program review is by comparison with similar forms of evaluation. Table 1 compares the key characteristics of formative reviews. These four reviews all differ in their purpose, the measures used, and the evaluators. An institutional review is undertaken primarily for improvement and development of the program; an accreditation review is undertaken often to meet the minimum standards of a discipline or profession. A state-level review may be undertaken primarily for purposes of accountability and efficient use of state resources. A performance review compares academic programs to other state programs and furnishes general evaluations regarding effectiveness.

Successful reviews are dynamic. That is, they are locally developed, implemented, and evaluated so that future reviews can be modified in accord with changing purposes. Reviews are not all conducted for the same purpose. They are conducted by various persons, at various times, for various reasons: program improvement, efficiency, effectiveness, termination, cost-effectiveness, and need. As we will see, successful reviews are individually designed to meet specific needs and purposes. There is no single paragon of program review. What works in one place at one time may well not work in a different place or time. Consequently, we believe in individually developed reviews based on the local environment, history, culture, needs, and the periodic evaluation of the process to ensure that it continues to respond to local needs.

The primary evaluators for an internal review are the faculty from the program. Although outside consultants might be used, they report to the faculty from the program being reviewed. In an accreditation review, the key evaluators come from the discipline or profession and are accountable to the accreditation organization representing the field of study. In state-level reviews, including those conducted by institutions, the reviewers are the state board staff or perhaps consultants who are accountable to the state board staff. In each case the evaluators differ in their orientation to the program and in their relative objectivity.

Guiding Principles

The objectives of program review are based on certain factors shown to be highly related to successful reviews. These objectives should be kept in mind while implementing the process described in the next several chapters. These objectives are:

- Fairness
- Comprehensiveness
- Timeliness
- Good communication
- Objectivity
- Credibility
- Utility

Few things can undermine the effectiveness of program review more than a process that is viewed as unfair either by those within an organization or those outside who must pass judgment on its effectiveness. One college president had a widely known dispute with a certain program and targeted it as one of the first to be reviewed. Consequently, all the

Table 1. Comparison of Accreditation and Institutional and State Program Reviews.

Feature	Institutional Reviews (Dept., School, College)	Accreditation Reviews (Professional and Regional)	State Coordinating Agency Reviews	Performance Reviews and Audits
Primary purpose	To develop programs, analyze their direction and content, assess their quality	To assess whether program or institution meets minimum standards	To evaluate the accountability and efficient use of state resources of an institution, program, or segment of postsecondary education vis-à-vis its peers	To evaluate the accountability and efficiency of a state program vis-à-vis other state programs; concerns only broad judgments about programs, not improvement or analysis
Primary measures	Indicators of quality deemed appropriate by institutional/ departmental personnel	Minimum approved standards of the discipline, state, or region (usually qualitative)	Input and outcome measures based on need, cost, productivity, and quality	Outcome measures based on program goals
Primary evaluators	Departmental or institutional personnel	Peer reviewers	Ranges from institutional self-reviewers to outside peers to extra institutional reviewers on agency staff, depending on state	Legislative or executive agency staffs

| Secondary evaluators | Peer consultants; advisory groups representing business, industry, or profession; current students and graduates | Departmental or institutional personnel via self-study | Program graduates, business or industry raters | Program graduates, industry or profession raters |

Source: Barak (1977).

programs in the first round of reviews quickly became known as being on the president's hit list. This experience at the outset tainted all reviews for a number of years and resulted in the trustees' refusal to back the administration on some of its recommendations because of all the mistrust created by the initial selection of programs to be reviewed. The effectiveness of the reviews was hampered until a new president eventually reestablished trust in the fairness of the review process.

In many instances, program review began because of a concern over graduate program quality in universities and in vocational education in community colleges. While few people would argue that these reviews were not needed, many were concerned that the exclusive focus on only a segment of an institution's programs would have a negative impact on the other programs. A dean in an eastern university commented that such a narrow focus resulted in an "unfortunate shifting of resources and emphasis from undergraduate programs to graduate programs." It is now recognized that successful reviews cover all programs at all levels in a comprehensive manner. Moreover, reviews should address all the needs of their audience so that multiple reviews are minimized.

Just as it is important to review all programs at all levels, it is essential to do so on a regular basis. Programs can change for the better or worse in a very short time. Faculty members, especially the highly regarded ones, move on to better positions and some retire; some resources improve and others become outdated. Consequently, there must be an effort to review programs regularly. In the typical cycle, every program is reviewed every five to six years on a regular schedule. The advantages to such an approach include the maintenance of a review structure (research personnel, review committees, and so on); opportunities to learn from the results of the previous cycle; and frequent assessment of progress. This does not necessarily mean that every program receives an in-depth evaluation, however, for it is possible to screen programs and then conduct in-depth reviews of those identified as problematic.

Not only do people like to be involved in developing things, they also like to be kept informed of what is happening. Otherwise they tend to lose interest or, even worse, begin to believe the rumors that inevitably spread in the absence of information. From the early stages of the needs assessment to the completion and meta-evaluation of the reviews, it is important to keep people informed, maintain a positive attitude, and ensure their support with a flow of information and status reports.

Webster defines being objective as "emphasizing the nature of reality as it is apart from personal reflections or feelings." It is important to build as much objectivity into the review process as is humanly possible. Care must be taken in the selection of personnel and procedures to ensure the appropriate degree of objectivity. People from the unit under review are likely to be the most knowledgeable persons regarding a program, but they are also likely to be the least objective. Peer reviewers who represent differing schools of thought or highly competitive programs may be objective in the sense that they are not part of the unit under review, but they too may have ulterior motives or axes to grind that make them less than objective. Care needs to be taken to assure that others who are perceived as more objective are involved in the reviews or that mechanisms are developed to compensate for the lack of objectivity.

Perhaps the single most important objective in developing a program review is to ensure credibility. The review process must be regarded as fair, objective, and reasonable. There must be built-in mechanisms to ensure that all programs are treated equally and that due process procedures are available. Reviews that are regarded as "witch-hunts," "stacked juries," and "kangaroo courts" can undermine their total effectiveness, especially when they are viewed as such by influential persons outside the organization.

Finally, people like to know that when they have worked hard on something, the effort has been worthwhile. Often a review's worth is judged by the use or nonuse of the results.

A Three-Stage Process

The three chapters that follow outline a process for the development, conduct, and evaluation of program review based on our experience and research. The outline and rationale for using each aspect are as follows.

Developing a Plan. In this first phase we provide the reader with a systematic approach to the development of a program review process. Like most endeavors, successful reviews stem from sound planning and execution. This step addresses the basic elements needed for the development of a program review plan. Many have found that extra effort in this developmental phase pays off in ensuring a strong process. Simply put, the end of a review is not the time to address design questions. Too many reviews are begun hastily in a crisis atmosphere, thus starting the process off on the wrong foot. We are not saying that reviews which follow the steps outlined here are going to be perfect, but they will avoid the major pitfalls. For those who are developing a program review process for the first time, preparing a plan should be the first step. For those who have a good idea of the purpose of their review and some idea how they plan to approach the task, a condensed version of a plan will be useful in defining the specifics of their approach. Those who feel their purpose is clear and their process sound may wish only to review Chapter Two as a checklist to assure that they are correct. In any event the purpose of developing a plan is to ensure a firm basis for the review.

Conducting the Review. This phase is the action stage of the review. Here the emphasis is on maintaining a proper climate. Many reviews go sour in this phase due to the way they are handled. On one campus, a faculty member described the climate as the "modern version of the inquisition." Chapter Three offers suggestions on how this type of climate can be avoided as well as positive suggestions for using consultants and analyzing the data. This information will be useful for the novice reviewer as well as the veteran since the overall climate has been a frequent source of criticism, consultants are more often misused than not, and data collection is frequently a major stumbling block in the review process.

Postreview. Postreview activities provide the finishing touches on the reviews, for nothing caps off a successful review better than a well-prepared report. Many reviews, however, fall flat at this stage. Those reviewing the results do not get a clear understanding of the process and the outcomes. Not only can this lead to misunderstanding at a time when consensus is needed, but the results may just be ignored. The two most common errors in the postreview phase are the lack of follow-up on recommendations and the failure to learn from mistakes and improve the review process for the next round of reviews. Chapter Four offers helpful suggestions to avoid these mistakes and presents steps for evaluating the review process.

Preparing for the Review

Once an institution has conducted a needs assessment as described in Chapter Two, it should prepare for the review process. As in any other new experience, people are anxious about the unknown. Administrators can ease this anxiety through education and involvement. Key leaders can become more knowledgeable about the process by attending seminars on program review and planning conducted by various professional organizations such as the Association of Institutional Research (AIR), the American Association of Higher Education (AAHE), the Association for the Study of Higher Education (ASHE), and the American Educational Research Association (AERA). Special seminars on program review and planning are also conducted by centers of higher education located at various research institutions across the United States and by the National Center for Higher Education Management Systems (NCHEMS). For more information about these programs, consult *The Chronicle for Higher Education,* which publishes a quarterly calendar of upcoming events in academia, or contact the organizations directly.

Additional preparation can be done by reviewing the literature and studying this handbook. The bibliography at the back of the book lists key articles related to specific aspects of program review. At a minimum, the major figures in the program review should be familiar with the contents of this book. Once the key elements of a successful review are understood, those involved in the process may consider meeting with various stakeholders to inform them of these key elements and allow them opportunities to participate. Key stakeholders include administrators, faculty, students, alumni, the governing boards, and community advisory groups.

Proper preparation of key figures in the program review is essential. Resources and time spent here are returned in triple later in the process. The preparation should ensure that people recognize what the review can accomplish and what it cannot. Certainly the program review will assist decision makers in making informed, credible, and fair judgments regarding a program's direction. It will *not* make the decision for them.

Summary

Program review is not a panacea for all the ills that confront higher education today. It is, however, a critical tool providing valuable information for strategic planning and decision making. Knowing a program's strengths and weaknesses is critical in determining its strategic direction. Focusing on a program's need for improvement is the first step toward excellence. A program review provides both the context and the process for conducting student assessments and then following up. In these and other ways, a program review contributes to an institution's overall improvement and accountability.

2

Planning for
an Effective Review

In a successful program review, as in other endeavors, people will support what they have helped create. Experience and the literature support the notion that the review process, and particularly the appropriate involvement of those affected by it, is a key factor in the eventual success of the total effort. The next three chapters provide detailed guidelines on the process of developing successful program reviews. The material presented suggests a number of options rather than a detailed checklist of things that must be done. Readers should choose those items that best fit their particular circumstances.

The first step in developing a successful program review begins with a needs assessment to determine whether program reviews are called for to address a particular need or problem. The needs assessment varies from a "quick and dirty" survey to an elaborate study. If a program review is sought, it is necessary to establish a climate for success and secure the approval of key figures. The needs assessment and conceptualization process are the primary focus of this chapter. Chapter Three covers the action phase of the review. Chapter Four covers the final report and its implementation. In total these three chapters represent a complete guide to the review of academic programs.

Step One: Identifying the Need for Review

To avoid developing a program review that is "dysfunctional," an organization should undertake a needs assessment. Put more positively, successful reviews require good design work to ensure that the process is viable and credible and addresses the needs that have been identified. The needs assessment is used to define the purposes, objectives, and needs with respect to a program review.

At most institutions, this step has not been formally or systematically undertaken. Only 6 percent or so of the colleges and universities we surveyed actually undertook an effort that could be described as a formal needs assessment. When queried further, however, most of the institutions mentioned the informal completion of many steps that would normally be included in a formal needs assessment. While not undertaken in a systematic fashion, these informal measures often achieved the same basic objectives. Consequently, whether one undertakes a formal or informal needs assessment is less important than whether or not certain key factors are taken into consideration. Mims (1978) cites the following factors to consider in conducting a needs assessment:

1. Key individuals and their appropriate levels of involvement
2. Problems to be addressed and likely solutions
3. Purposes and objectives to be served and the measurement of their achievement
4. Critical factors to be considered and appropriate strategies for their consideration
5. Constraints (such as deadlines, collective bargaining, personnel, resources) and their likely impact
6. Various alternative approaches to program review and their likely impact on the organization

Some of these factors are discussed in the next two chapters; the rest are examined here. It should go without saying that key players should be involved in any effort that will have a major impact on the institution. Yet one of the most common mistakes made in developing program reviews is the failure to involve key people in the effort. Part of the difficulty stems from the definition of "key" people and their "involvement." Unfortunately there are no hard and fast rules to help. Institutions of higher education differ so greatly, even within the same state, that standardized guidelines would create as many problems as they attempt to solve. The task of identifying key figures is not impossible, however, and some help can be gleaned from the practices of others as reported in the results of our 1986 survey (Barak, 1986).

It should come as no surprise to anyone in higher education that our survey results reported that the most common way to undertake a needs assessment is to appoint a committee. The second most common form is the administrative team, and the third is the use of consultants. The committee has the advantage of broad participation and local perspective. The administrative team usually has the advantage of better support services and more involvement from key leaders. Consultants often have the advantage of experience, broad perspective on the issues, objectivity, knowledge of program review alternatives, and frankness.

Among the disadvantages of committees are their lack of control over results, the amount of time consumed, and the slow pace; as well, they often lack experience and knowledge of program review. The disadvantages of administrators relate to the lack of participative involvement, suspicion over motives, and, because of other duties, the lack of adequate time to devote to the task. The disadvantages of consultants are their cost and their lack of knowledge about the institution.

Usually the best approach is one that combines all these figures in a task force in order to gain widespread involvement over the shortest period of time. A typical needs assessment committee would include key faculty members (faculty senate, important committee chairs, respected faculty), institutional research staff, academic administrators and staff (appropriate to the level of review), and business office staff. Students, faculty union leaders, consultants, trustees, and presidents are sometimes included as well. It is advisable to involve only a few people representing these various groups, but institutional practice and the need to involve key figures are major considerations. New patterns of involvement should be considered with caution, since a needs assessment committee is not the place to plow new ground in organizational politics. A workable group generally has no more than twelve members. Only those deemed essential to the effort should serve on the committee. Others may serve in subgroups or in an advisory capacity, commenting on proposals and so on.

The committee mix includes persons with knowledge of the organization's structure, its processes, data bases, finances, academic affairs, political environment, and program reviews. These people should be widely known and highly regarded. A balance of political and technical expertise is desirable.

To convey the importance of organizational support for the needs assessment, the committee should be appointed by someone at the top of the institution's structure, such as the chancellor, president, or chief academic officer. Many institutions report that when the appointment is made public throughout the organization, it helps set the right tone for the effort. One caution about publicity is in order, however. The appointment should be accompanied by a positive yet honest description of the program review to be undertaken.

The appointments should be accompanied, too, by a list of specific charges to the committee and a timetable appropriate to the task. Often insufficient time is allotted to the job or, at the other extreme, no timetable is provided, resulting in an ad hoc committee that becomes entrenched and involved in continuous debate. Ideally, sufficient time should be allotted to undertake the assigned task, yet not so much time that people lose sight of their goals. The average review with self-studies and outside consultants takes about one academic year. Heydinger (1978) notes: "If institutional consensus currently exists and if the purposes for program review have already been articulated, then the task of assessing needs may be straightforward. However, if this needs assessment requires interfacing with many constituencies and balancing the needs of many groups, then the faculty or staff responsible for executing the needs assessment should be released from some of their current responsibilities. This demonstrates the institution's commitment to the task" (p. 6).

A chair with good interpersonal skills and knowledge of the task at hand should be appointed at the same time. The specific charge to the committee provides the direction it needs to complete its task. Such a charge will vary from place to place depending on the review's specific purpose, but it should address the following basic concerns:

1. What problems and issues underlie the decision to undertake a program review?
2. Is a program review the appropriate answer or even a partial answer at this time to these problems and issues?
3. Are there more viable alternatives to address these problems and issues?

The question of feasibility must also be addressed:

1. What purposes are to be served by the review? By what criteria will its achievement be judged?
2. What are the various approaches to a program review? What are their relative advantages and disadvantages?
3. What are the critical needs of those interested in the review?
4. Are there adequate resources (people, money, equipment) to mount and sustain the effort?
5. What is the timetable for the review? Is it adequate for the objectives being sought?
6. What are the constraints to achieving the desired results? [Heydinger, 1978, p. 7]

These basic considerations are suggested because consultants have more than once been confronted with situations in which the problems and issues do not really relate to program review. One board of trustees sought help initially to review programs, for example, but after considerable discussion it became clear that some administrative changes would meet their needs.

In determining the need for a program review Heydinger (1978) suggests that consideration be given to institutional climate, resource requirements, and institutional benefits. He recommends a review of the institution's readiness to implement a program review, the commitment of administrators to allocate the necessary resources, and an examination of the benefits that are expected to accrue from program review. These benefits should be viewed in light of the resources to be expended (pp. 9–11).

If program review *is* what is being sought, then it becomes necessary to consider its feasibility. In practice everything from a rough overview of the desired process to a detailed flowchart itemizing each step has been used to meet the requirements of this stage. It is best to have only a general overview since those who will consider the committee's recommendations may want to modify the overall process design, and persons other than the committee members may need to be involved in the detailed process. In general the process recommended by the needs assessment committee should consist of only an overview outlining the approach and its major components: who is involved, their general responsibilities, the types of programs to be reviewed, the timing of the reviews, and the staff and resources needed.

In gathering information the committee should, if time and resources permit, look broadly at both internal and external constituents of the organization. Some subunits of the organization may already be conducting reviews, for example, and may be hesitant in relating their experience. All of the usual data-gathering techniques should be considered including literature searches, interviews, and surveys. If the organization has a previous history of review efforts, it should be documented and evaluated.

Many committees solicit information on processes that others have implemented at their institution or agency. Such information has limited usefulness and should be reviewed with caution. Some administrators are fond of bragging about their program reviews and often tend to exaggerate their success. Moreover, a process that is successful at one organization will rarely work elsewhere without modifications (usually major modifications). Consultants frequently are called in to repair damage resulting from the adoption of someone else's process. Information on another organization's process is only useful in terms of demonstrating types of approaches and general concepts. There is no perfect model of program review—only many different ones that work in certain circumstances (Barak, 1986). A good consultant will not push one approach but will list a range of viable alternatives.

The end product of the needs assessment should be a written report that responds to each charge of the committee and provides an overview of the proposed review process (assuming that the committee concludes that a program review is both necessary and feasible). This report should present the committee's assessment of the likely results of implementing the program review and should include any other recommendations needed to ensure the review's success. Essentially the report should say yes or no to the feasibility of undertaking a program review; if the conclusion is yes, it should sketch the process to be considered. Like other reports by study groups, this report should be acted on in an objective and timely manner by organizational decision makers.

The final aspect of the needs assessment involves establishing a climate conducive for conducting a successful review. It is primarily a communication task in that this is the step where support for the review is secured. The outcomes of the design phase need to be conveyed to decision makers and their support secured. Any recommendations for the proposed process should be approved or implemented— by assigning duties to staff, for example, or by allocating resources.

The next step is the broad task of securing support and providing information to the organization and the community at large. The primary need for communication, however, is internal. Those who will be affected by the review should be familiar with the entire process. Information can take the form of a newsletter for those within the organization, or the proposal can be explained in a series of hearings. It should be made clear that these meetings, unlike the hearings suggested during the needs assessment and design phases, are not for the purpose of seeking additional comments and suggestions. Rather, their purpose is primarily informational. This does not mean that good suggestions or serious problems uncovered in the informational hearing should be ignored: Good suggestions should be taken into consideration at the appropriate time; flaws in the process should be corrected.

Step Two: Beginning a Program Review Plan

The second step in designing a program review involves the overall conceptualization of the review process, the defining of tasks and roles, and the establishment of timetables for completion of the various tasks and the process itself. This phase will result in a plan for the review. It builds on the accomplishments of the first phase and is perhaps the single most important aspect of program review since it determines *who* will be involved in the review, *what* their role will be, *when* the review will take place, and *how* the review will be conducted.

Overall Design Considerations. There is more than one way to conduct a successful program review. While a variety of approaches have been used and the potential exists for the use of many others, the general approach suggested here is consistent with successful practices we have encountered in our research and in our experience in the field. Those interested in exploring new approaches should consult some of the general descriptions that have been published (Madaus, Scriven, and Stufflebeam, 1983; House, 1986; Stufflebeam and Shinkfield, 1985; Trochim, 1986; Worthen and Sanders, 1987).

There is no general consensus regarding the "best" process to follow. One review of the literature concluded that the only point of agreement among evaluation experts was that "all evaluations should include a certain amount of interaction between evaluators and their audiences at the outset of the evaluation to identify evaluation needs, and at its conclusion to communicate its findings" (Nevo, 1986, p. 36). In between these beginning and terminating points are a number of other activities where a great deal of discretion is possible. The design considerations presented here reflect options. The wise designer will select those that best fit the review's environment and purposes.

Criteria. Having defined the purpose, the desired results, and the expected uses of the reviews in the first phase of the needs assessment, it is now necessary to develop specific aspects of the reviews. A key aspect is determining the criteria by which the program will be judged. Depending on the size, nature, and composition of the group undertaking the design task, one or more of the following techniques can be used to define the criteria for the program review: small-group discussion, large-group discussion, surveys (Delphi type), copying from others, professional consultant expertise, and administrative decision.

Whichever approach is used, the basic task is to develop a list of criteria of significance to the review of academic programs. The next step is to refine the list by eliminating redundancies and sharpening the focus of each remaining criterion until there is a reasonable consensus that the list addresses the major aspects of an academic program and key figures are reasonably satisfied with the list. One approach that has met with frequent success involves the use of a modified Delphi technique consisting of several steps. These include:

1. A general questionnaire asking those involved to list the criteria by which they think the programs should be reviewed.
2. A review of the lists to eliminate duplicate criteria and group the remaining criteria into major types such as those related to quality, cost, centrality, need/demand, productivity, outcomes, and so on. This step is helpful in

ensuring that the criteria are comprehensive and address all aspects of a program consistent with the purposes of the review.

3.   A ranking of the remaining criteria from most important to least important. A review of the rankings usually reveals a degree of consensus that some criteria are more important than others. This information can be used to reduce the size of the list if it is thought to be too long or ambitious. It can also be used as the beginning step to develop weights for each criterion that might be used in ranking the results of the program review. If a weighing system is desired, successive steps in which the criteria are further refined and ranked may be necessary.

This approach is detailed here to underscore the importance of selecting the relevant criteria. The method has had a good record of success. This success is in no small way related to the fact that it engages the active involvement of persons critical to the ultimate success of the program review. Involvement gives participants a sense of ownership in the process and helps assure their support of the overall effort.

Indicators of Criteria. The task of finding indicators for each criterion is often more difficult than selection of the criteria because of the complexity of the task. First, only indicators that are specific and distinct should be selected. This does not mean that the indicator should be limited to quantitative data. Good qualitative measures are available and should be included as indicators where appropriate. Second, not all of the criteria may be easily and accurately expressed in measurable terms. Some will need to be dropped and others substituted to meet local needs. There may also be disagreement over which are the best indicators of a particular criterion. A third complexity is the availability of data on each of the desired indicators. Some of the criteria may, in fact, be indicators of a broader criterion, and these will need to be determined. Sometimes it is helpful to write evaluation questions based on the indicators. (What does this indicator seek to answer?) Because of these complexities, some have found that the task is best accomplished with the assistance of experts who know the field and the available data bases. These experts could be staff members involved in institutional research and data base management.

The indicators are of two types. First, there are indicators that are descriptive or quantifiable such as cost per student credit hour and number of graduates over a given period of time. Second, there are indicators that are less specific and more qualitative such as adequacy of facilities and equipment, peer ratings, and assessment of leadership. It is often useful to segregate these two types to facilitate analysis and decision making later on.

Sources such as Clark, Harnett, and Baird (1976) are helpful in providing useful indicators. Many, if not most, indicators will have to be developed locally to meet the needs of a particular review and the available data. If there is a need to undertake a cost/benefit or cost/effectiveness analysis, for example, it might be necessary to develop indicators that take account of multiple outcomes, imperfect information, and lack of decision makers' proficiency in cost studies. Some help can be gained in this effort by developing a matrix chart with the proposed indicators arrayed by criterion down the left margin and data availability questions along the top. Each proposed indicator is checked against the data questions to ascertain its potential for use in the program review. An example of this technique is provided in Table 2.

The criteria for the selection of indicators include:

1. Responsiveness to the needs and purposes of the review
2. Cost and cost-effectiveness of data collection and analysis
3. Simplicity so they can be readily understood by those associated with the review
4. Validity to ensure that the indicators represent a valid proxy for the criteria
5. Comprehensiveness to ensure there are sufficient indicators to provide a well-rounded picture of a program

Table 2. Example of Matrix for Indicator Feasibility.

Type?	Audience Need?	Source?	Criterion Reference?	Cost of Collection?	Logistical Problems?	Historical Trend?	Problems of Summarization?	Display of Data?
Descriptive								
• Average salaries								
• Direct operating expenses								
• Student credit hours								
• Number of graduates								
• Cost/student credit hour								
Judgmental								
• Adequacy of facilities								
• Adequacy of support staff								
• Adequacy of competitive salary								
• Assessment of leadership								
• Peer ratings								

6. Reliability to ensure that they accurately reflect what they purport to represent
7. Credibility to ensure that the review itself is not brought into question
8. Objectivity to avoid the data bias
9. Uniformity so that data from all programs reviewed are reasonably consistent
10. Relevance to ensure a meaningful effort

Sometimes it is useful to assign numerical weights to each of the indicators. Assigning weights allows one to quantify the review results and enables comparisons of various programs. This approach is more successfully implemented in community colleges than in four-year colleges and research universities. In Table 3, for example, a program's cost-effectiveness is assigned a numerical weight as would all the indicators used in the review. Figure 1 shows the graphic results of such an effort.

Data about academic programs can come from many sources. The program itself is the most obvious source. Data are also available from institutional, state, and national data bases such as the U.S. Department of Education Integrated

Figure 1. Graph of Numerical Weighted Indicators.

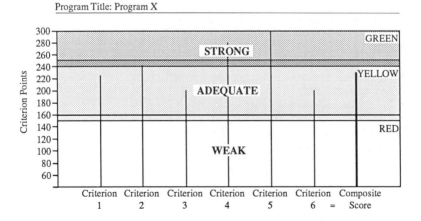

Program Title: Program X

Table 3. Examples of Criterion Weights.

Criterion	Paired-Comparison Weight	Proportional Weight
Program's cost-effectiveness	-0.563	100(1 - 0.563)/6 = 7
Program's success in terms of student performance	0.462	100(1 + 0.462)/6 = 24

Postsecondary Education Data System (IPEDS); faculty salary information can be obtained from the American Association of University Professors (AAUP). Many reviewers think it is useful to compile an inventory of all related data as suggested in Table 2. During the development of program review indicators, it may be necessary to modify, augment, and create new data bases on programs. A good discussion of institutional data bases is provided in Sharp (1988). Tables 4 and 5 show typical data indicators for two possible criteria (in this case, productivity and need).

Table 4. Examples of Productivity Indicators.

Program enrollments
• Five-year credit-hour enrollments
• Five-year headcount enrollments
Program completion
• Number of degrees and certificates granted over five years
• Proportion of starters completing the program over x years
Faculty productivity
• Student-faculty ratio
• Class size
Program costs
• Discipline costs/state average
• Program costs/institutional average
Graduate outcomes
• Number and percentage of graduates obtaining full-time employment in the field
• Number and percentage of graduates passing professional qualifying exams over a five-year period
• Test scores on graduation exams over a period of years

Table 5. Examples of Program Need Indicators.

Local/regional/national job market needs
• Number of existing and projected job openings
• Proportion of local employers expressing need for program

Support of academic/occupational area
• Participation in program advisory committee meeting
• Proportion of credits accepted at other institutions

Success in meeting student needs
• Proportion of completers/leavers satisfied with instruction in program

Program autonomy
• Proportion of total program credit hours by program faculty
• Service instruction to other programs

Lack of duplication with other programs
• Enrollment of similar programs in region
• Number of other courses in same discipline taught at institution

---

Those who are conducting their first program review tend to collect too much information. Consequently, caution is urged here to avoid "data overload," a condition in which the reviewers find themselves incapable of effectively analyzing the information because of its quantity. As a general rule of thumb, three to six good indicators of each major criterion (such as cost, quality of faculty and students, need/demand, centrality of mission, and productivity) with good supporting data and a strong consensus on their use will often suffice.

Basic Approaches. The preceding sections have noted the variances resulting from the different review approaches. Here we consider the most commonly used approaches. The costs of the reviews should be kept in mind in reading the discussion that follows.

We do not use the word *model* in discussing the various approaches because there are no ideal approaches. The word also seems to imply that if one could get hold of a "model" it could be implemented at any institution with success. These common misconceptions can lead to unfortunate results, for they ignore two fundamental principles: Reviews should be individually designed and planned to address the needs, purposes, and structure of a particular situation; reviews are most successful if the people affected by them have been involved in their development. Consultants hired to fix dysfunctional reviews find more often than not that one or both of these guidelines have been ignored. In some cases severe damage has been done to the programs and the reviews.

There are five basic types of program review: consultant-oriented reviews; survey-oriented reviews; data-oriented reviews; self-study reviews; and some combination thereof. Table 6 shows the key characteristics of these five approaches.

Consultant-Oriented Reviews. The consultant-oriented reviews have as their primary feature evaluation by outside consultants. They are widely used because they solicit the expertise of someone knowledgeable about a given field. The ultimate success of these reviews depends on the quality of the consultants and their ability to prepare useful reports and recommendations. Selecting the right people to conduct the review is critical. A person may be outstanding in his or her field and yet be unable to evaluate a program properly. Successful reviews of this type generally observe the following guidelines:

1. People from the unit being reviewed should have a role in selecting the consultants. They know their programs better than anyone. If the review is summative, this usually means they suggest the names of possible consultants. Further names can be obtained from others in the field, from learned societies, and from others with experience in using consultants for this purpose. If the review is formative, the unit's faculty will probably be heavily involved in the selection process.
2. The consultants should be screened to ascertain their experience in evaluating programs. The committee should particularly check references on prior review activities.
3. The consultants should be selected, hired, and given explicit instructions by someone outside of the unit being reviewed if the review is summative.

Table 6. Five Common Approaches to Program Review.

Feature	Consultant-Oriented	Survey-Oriented	Data-Oriented	Self-Study	Combination
Purpose	Summative or formative	Summative or formative	Usually summative	Usually formative	Summative
Primary persons	Consultants	Institutional research person	Institutional research person	Program faculty	Review committee or administrator
Typical methods	Expert opinions of consultants	Survey instruments	Data collection and analysis	Self-study	Survey consultants, data analysis, self-study
Typical questions	What is consultant's opinion of the program?	What are student, faculty, alumni, employees', others' opinions of the program?	What do the data indicate about the effectiveness and efficiency of the program?	What do we want to know about ourselves and our program?	All of the other questions
Cost	High	Low-medium	Medium-high	Low	Medium-high
Resource requirements	Low	Medium	Medium-high	Low	Medium-high
Design considerations	Requires careful selection and instructions for consultants	Requires careful development, distribution, and analysis of surveys	Requires careful development of data elements, indicators, and analysis	Requires careful design of self-study, contact, and analysis of results	All of the other considerations

4. The consultants' schedule should be worked out in advance so their time is not wasted. There should be flexibility in the schedule to allow time for unexpected needs. They should not just be allowed to wander aimlessly at will.
5. The visits for summative reviews should be professionally oriented; social events should be limited to scheduled meals.
6. The consultants' instructions should spell out the purpose of the visit, expectations, guidelines on conduct, the availability of staff assistance during and after the visit, pay and reimbursement of expenses, and the deadline for the final report. (Some do not get part or all of their compensation until the report is received.) Most important, the instructions should specify the kind of review that is being sought.

Survey-Oriented Reviews. These reviews have as their primary feature the use of surveys to ascertain perspectives on the program as reported by faculty, students, alumni, and employers. The survey instrument can be either self-developed or commercially developed. Commercial surveys have several advantages: They have been developed, field tested, and printed, thus saving considerable time and expense; most have been developed with extensive involvement of experts in the field, thus allowing for more rigor and credibility; some have data bases that can provide comparative data relating to the program being reviewed; some have been revised as a result of extensive use in the field; some allow local questions to be inserted to meet the specific needs of a given review. Apart from the question of cost, commercial surveys have another disadvantage: They may not meet local needs as well as a locally developed instrument.

      Certain factors have been found helpful in the development and selection of survey instruments. First, it is important to distinguish between evaluation and research. Research is aimed at gaining knowledge; evaluations are intended for purposes of decision making (program improvement, effectiveness, efficiency, and so on). Second, it is useful to know that many who use a survey-oriented approach feel that more than one instrument is needed as the same instrument cannot effectively survey faculty, students, and alumni, for example. Third, it is important to keep in mind what is going to be evaluated, what questions the evaluation will answer, and what decisions are likely to be made as a result of this review. If this is done, the intent of a commercial instrument will closely match the purpose of the review.

If a survey-oriented approach is used, one person or office should have the responsibility for development, pretesting, mailing, follow-up, collecting, and analysis. Usually this is the institutional research and analysis unit. The importance of accuracy in wording and analysis requires that these tasks be undertaken by experts in the field. Many self-developed survey instruments produce meaningless results due to ambiguous or biased questions and are difficult to analyze.

Data-Oriented Reviews. These reviews have as their main feature the collection and analysis of both quantitative and qualitative data on the programs being reviewed. They can be divided further into two types in which (1) the entire review is based on data collection, review, and analysis and (2) the data review acts as a screening process to identify programs needing a closer review using other approaches such as consultants and surveys (Barak and Berdahl, 1978; Barak, 1982a).

The primary requirements of this approach are a comprehensive and sophisticated data base and competent staff for data management and analysis. Careful effort must also be given to the development of data elements and indicators for this approach. Those who will be affected by the results must be involved in the development and application of the data elements and indicators. The approach offers an alternative to those who do not want to review all programs in depth on a regular schedule. By screening programs regularly, it is possible to pinpoint problem programs and subject only these to an in-depth review.

Criticism of this approach is directed mainly at the quality of the data, its availability, and the lack of expert judgment. Perfect data are difficult to obtain. The lack of expert judgment—that is, someone "who knows the field"—makes some people dissatisfied with this approach, and people from the units reviewed will use this argument if the data review is critical of their program. To get around this problem some have had "experts" review the data and help design the survey instruments. Involving faculty in the development of the review process also helps.

Self-Study Reviews. These reviews are usually of the formative type and focus on the improvement of programs. The primary persons responsible are the program faculty, although the guidelines for the self-study content may be prescribed. Kells (1983) provides an excellent guide to self-studies and formative reviews that details the entire process.

Combination Reviews. These reviews are probably the most common approach because they tend to mix and match one or more of the other types to meet the specific needs of the institution conducting the review. Generally they consist of a self-study developed by the program faculty, surveys or interviews of students (and less frequently faculty, alumni, and employees), the use of outside consultants, and the analysis of relevant data.

Step Three: Assigning Responsibility

It is important to assign duties and responsibility for the review in order to avoid confusion and breakdowns in the process. This step basically involves the question of *who* is responsible for *what*. Here, as in other aspects of design, it is necessary to base the assignments on the local situation and individual talents as well as on the purpose of the review. Table 7 shows typical levels of responsibility for various persons and groups associated with the review.

Table 7. Typical Levels of Responsibility and Involvement.

Persons/ Groups	Review Conducted for Program	Review Conducted for Department	Review Conducted for School/College	Review Conducted for Institution	Review Conducted for System	Review Conducted for State
Faculty from program	High	Low/ medium/high	Low/ medium/high	Low/ medium/high	None	None
Faculty outside of program but within institution	Low	High	High	High	Low	Low/none
Faculty outside of institution	Low/ medium/high	Low/ medium/high	Medium/high	Medium/high	Medium/high	Medium/high
Students	Low	Low	Low	Low	Low	Low
Alumni	Low/medium	Low	Low	Low/medium	Low/medium	Low/ medium/high
Employers of program's alumni	Low/medium	Low/medium	Low/medium	Low/medium	Low/medium	Low
Advisory groups to program	Low/medium	Low/medium	Low/medium	Low/medium	Low	Low

Table 7. Typical Levels of Responsibility and Involvement, Cont'd.

Persons/ Groups	Review Conducted for Program	Review Conducted for Department	Review Conducted for School/College	Review Conducted for Institution	Review Conducted for System	Review Conducted for State
Administrators from department with program	Low	High	Low	Low	Low	Low
Administrators from college or school	Low	Low	High	Medium	Low	None
Experts in field	Low/medium	Low/medium	Low/medium	Low/medium	Low/ medium/high	Low/ medium/high
Process consultants	Low	Low	Low	Low	Low	Low
Administrators (institutional level)	Low	Low	Low	High	Medium	Low
Administrators (system or district level)	None	None	Low	Low	High	Low
State Coordinating Governing Board staff	None	None	None	None/low	Low	High

Trustees	Low	Low	Low	Low/medium/high	Low	Low
State Coordinating Governing Board members	None	None	None	Low	None	High
Institutional research persons	Low/medium	Low/medium	Low/medium	Low/medium	Low/medium	Low/medium

Generally the level of involvement for various persons in academic program reviews depends on the locus of responsibility and the type of review. The specific tasks these persons will perform again depend on the review's nature and purpose as well as the institutional environment. Typical responsibilities of key participants are summarized here for formative reviews:

- Faculty: design the review; do the self-study; hire consultants; collect the data; survey students, employers, and alumni and generally supervise the reviews; analyze data; write the report; implement recommendations
- Administrators: be interviewed or surveyed

For summative reviews the following duties are typical:

- Faculty in the program being reviewed: suggest consultants; undertake the self-study; assist in review and collection of data
- Faculty outside the program: serve on review committee; hire consultants; collect and analyze data; survey students, alumni, and employees; oversee reviews; write the final report and make recommendations
- Line administrators: hire consultants; appoint the review committee; design the process; write reports; review recommendations and take steps for their implementation
- Staff administrators: collect and analyze data; assist in interpreting data
- Students and alumni: be interviewed or surveyed

These duties may vary from institution to institution. Generally research universities are the most collegial in their review efforts: Considerable responsibility is delegated to faculty committees, and administrative roles tend to involve general monitoring rather than direct supervision. In comprehensive universities and four-year colleges this characterization is somewhat less true. In two-year colleges and proprietary institutions there is considerably more adminis-

Figure 2. Collegiality of Reviews by Institutions.

Collegial◄							►Authoritative
(high faculty involve- ment)	Private Research University	Public Research University	4-Year College	Compre- hensive Univer- sity	Com- munity College	Proprie- tary Institu- tion	(high adminis- trative involve- ment)

trative involvement: They are less collegial to the extent that the program faculty has only a minimal role in the review (see Figure 2).

Step Four: Determining Resource Requirements

The resources needed for a program review depend on the review's nature and purposes. If the review is an in-house formative study using existing data, minimal resources will be needed. If, however, the review is to be a summative study with external consultants involving considerable data collection and analysis, the resource requirements are likely to be extensive.

The resource requirements should be estimated as part of the needs assessment to ensure that they can be made available. The major resource requirements (human and otherwise) include:

- Data collection and analysis
- Faculty, staff, and administrative time
- External consultants
- Travel and expenses
- Printing and postage

The direct cost of conducting a program review ranges from $1,000 to $50,000 per year. The more extensive the effort, the higher the cost. The use of outside consultants generally adds considerably to the cost and ranges from $200 to $500 (plus expenses) per consulting day. A typical visit consists of one to three days on campus and one or two days for report writing. Surveys of faculty, staff, and alumni using standardized instruments cost several thousand dollars (plus postage per person). Homemade surveys would be less expensive but have certain disadvantages noted elsewhere in this chapter.

Step Five: Scheduling

Program reviews are typically conducted every five years. At the institutional, system, and state levels this means that one-fifth of the programs are being reviewed every year. Some programs, because of unique circumstances, may take more than a year to review while a few may take less than a year. On average a well-planned process can complete a review of the typical program within the academic school year.

The specific programs reviewed in a given year are selected on the following basis: random selection; urgent problems (such as loss of accreditation); change in administration; by academic unit (such as colleges or schools); in response to state mandate; or to fit the schedule of other evaluations (such as accreditation). The last reason is particularly important because we have often heard complaints from faculty and staff that they are being overburdened with various evaluations that seem to consume more and more of their time. This evaluation overkill can often be avoided by timing various evaluations wisely and combining them where possible. All six purposes noted above constitute legitimate reasons for selection. Occasionally programs are selected on the basis of an administrative hit list. Such an approach runs the risk of jeopardizing the entire review effort as all the reviews become associated with dire connotations. The result is morale problems for the faculty and students associated with the program and a defensive attitude that can disrupt the review process.

When all aspects of the review process are decided upon it is usually helpful to diagram the entire process to see that all the components have been addressed and the process flows smoothly from beginning to end. The plan should then be checked to ensure its adequacy:

- Is the review clearly focused? Are the who, what, why, and when adequately described?
- Will the review provide the information needed for decision making?
- Is the information adequate? Are there procedures available to answer the review questions? Does the information collected relate to the needs of the review? Are the data available? Are there procedures for disseminating, reporting, and interpreting the results of the review?
- Is the reporting adequate? To whom will the report be submitted? Will reports be timely and effective? Is it feasible to complete the evaluation in the allotted time?
- Are there plans to evaluate the reviews after the first cycle? By what criteria will the success of the review be judged? Are there credibility problems?

Summary

The needs assessment should result in a carefully developed plan that essentially spells out in detail who will be involved in the reviews, what their roles will be, when the reviews will take place, and how they will be conducted. According to Mims (1978, pp. 14-15), the needs assessment should result in seven basic outcomes:

1. A statement of purposes, expected results, and expected uses
2. Criteria for judging results of the review process and for judging the design of specific reviews
3. Specification of administrative responsibilities and policies for conducting reviews and distributing results, monitoring implementation, and providing information
4. Design policies and guidelines
5. Procedures for identifying new information needs, updating review plans, and evaluating the review process itself
6. Resource requirements (staff and dollars)
7. A summary schedule of program reviews

The plan resulting from the design effort needs formal or informal approval by the administrative leadership. Most reviewers insist that the plan should have support from key figures to ensure its acceptance within the organization. Preferably it will be a formal, public approval. In any case, there must be strong support for the plan at the outset. Later on, when debate gets heated, it will be too late to find that the effort lacks strong support. Acceptance is a key step in creating a conducive environment for the reviews to take place. This aspect, sometimes called "creating the climate," puts the reviews in their most positive light and in the process helps assure cooperation.

This is also a good time to disseminate copies of the plan in draft form to provide an opportunity for review and comment. Some have found that holding informational hearings helps to create a conducive climate. Appointments to review committees and the assignment of specific responsibilities are also made at this time so that everyone affected will know where to address their questions and concerns. Good communication always helps in reducing fears and rumors about being evaluated.

3

Conducting the Review

Just as the conditions for young seedlings need to be carefully monitored to ensure proper growth and development, the proper conditions must be established and then maintained for successful program reviews. Appropriate persons must be kept informed, reviews accepted, consultants coordinated, and data analyzed. These are all activities associated with the coordination of the reviews. The realities of everyday life on campuses affect program reviews just as they affect promotion, tenure, and budgets. Above all, political realities are important to the actual conduct of the review.

Colleges and universities are carefully constructed coalitions of power that operate primarily through consensus. Since program reviews affect resource allocations—that is, as a result of a program review some programs are likely to receive more resources and some programs less—this shifting of resources also shifts the balance of power within the institution, creating tension and turmoil. If resources are reallocated as a result of a program review, new coalitions of power must be constructed for the organization to be effective.

Successful program reviews facilitate the shifting of power because the process is clearly understood by all involved, the results are openly discussed, and the reallocation of resources is viewed as best for the institution. Administrators need to anticipate this shift in the balance of power and ensure that new coalitions are formed. This can be done in several ways. First, the program review process and its outcomes must have top-level support from the deans through the president. These key figures must be assured that although the balance of power may shift with the resources, their institution will still fulfill its mission. Deans particularly need to be assured that their units will still have a vital role in the institution's mission.

Second, the institution and its leaders must make a long-range commitment to program review and planning. Too often a program review is initiated as a means to meet some budgetary constraint. Once that constraint has been lifted, the institution forgoes program review and planning. As noted earlier, programs change, faculty changes, and institutions change. Without an ongoing review and planning process, institutions will base their decisions on historical precedent, tradition, and individual preference.

Finally, administrators can ensure a successful program review by stressing its positive outcomes. Too often the review is blamed for events that may or may not be related to the process. At one school of education that had undertaken an extensive program review, several influential faculty members left in one year. The program review was frequently cited by remaining faculty as the reason why their colleagues left. The truth was that each faculty member left for individual reasons totally unrelated to program review. In fact, they had been looking for other positions for some time. Administrators should make a point of stressing the accomplishments of program review: what programs were strengthened, what resources were garnered, and what information was gained. One discontinued program involving a faculty member and eight students needs to be weighed against the needs of the total faculty and student body. A successful program review will demonstrate its usefulness and effectiveness early, but administrators cannot assume that everyone will readily see its positive effects. The political impact of program review can be minimized by building a conducive climate.

Establishing the Proper Climate

Establishing the proper organizational climate usually consists of four steps:

1. Gaining the acceptance and strong support of key decision makers
2. Establishing and maintaining good communications
3. Obtaining necessary resources
4. Implementing and coordinating the program review plan

In every situation where program reviews are being implemented, there are persons in authority whose support and commitment are imperative for its success. These people must be identified and their approval and support sought. While the specific individuals will vary depending on local circumstances, they generally include the administrative head of the unit encompassed by the review. On one campus, for example, the key figures included the president, the vice-presidents for academic and business affairs, the deans of the colleges, and a very dynamic board of trustees chair who had a special interest in program review. On another campus, the president's approval was sufficient. One particularly effective state review process obtained the support of key political and institutional leaders before being implemented. In all of these instances, the leaders' support was obtained after they had been given at least one opportunity to comment on the proposed program review. Without such support it might have been difficult to sell the review to others. In addition, the whole process might have broken down as individual programs were reviewed and recommendations for their future developed.

There is a strong feeling among experienced reviewers that the formal support of decision makers is desirable but not critical. Formal support can be obtained through such mechanisms as a resolution by the board of trustees, an open letter to the campus, a public announcement, or a speech to the faculty senate by an appropriate decision maker or

a highly respected faculty member. A good in-house public relations office can be instrumental in facilitating this
communication.

It is also wise to obtain the support of those affected by
the review plan such as faculty, staff, students, and others.
They need to know what the reviews are, their purpose, how
they were developed, how they will be implemented, and the
anticipated outcomes. Especially important to the success of
the reviews are the general communication effort and rumor
control. More often than not there is a good deal of uneasiness
associated with being reviewed. Students and faculty have
been known to feel threatened by reviews and to react in
strange ways. In an ideal climate they should be committed
to the reviews, not threatened. Some reviewers have found it
helpful to meet with groups of faculty and students separately
to discuss their concerns and assure them that the process
will be fair, that they will have an opportunity to contribute,
that they will have a chance to review the final report, and
that they will be kept informed of any significant activities as
the reviews progress. Various mechanisms have been used to
provide this information: newsletters, memorandums, open
hearings on campus, opportunities for review and comment
on drafts, campus meetings and statewide meetings, announce-
ments, presentations to faculty governance groups and student
organizations, and training sessions.

Although it is difficult to say just who should be kept
informed in a particular situation, given the variety and complexity of higher education, a few examples should provide
some guidance. One community college's failure to involve
and inform program advisory groups resulted in significant,
and eventually successful, opposition to recommendations
coming out of the reviews. On a major research university
campus, misinformed alumni stopped a merger proposal
resulting from a program review. In both of these instances,
the people responsible for the review later realized their mis-
take: Failing to inform and gain the support of key figures is
a major failure in communication.

Part of the difficulty lies in knowing exactly who

should be kept informed. As a general rule of thumb, it pays to be particularly sensitive to the audiences related to each program being reviewed whether it be a profession, industry, or just people with a special interest in the area. People close to the program can help identify these key persons. Such contacts may not always be helpful in preventing opposition later on, but they at least begin the process of communication and can minimize the damage since they themselves had a part in the reviews. This approach is often more judicious than trying to explain why they were never informed.

While initial support for the review effort is essential, continuing support is equally important. Program reviews often take a year or more to complete, so considerable time passes between the initial information and the final report and recommendations. Many have found this gap too long, since it often results in opportunities for counterproductive rumors to spread. Some have found that these unfortunate developments can be prevented or at least minimized through the establishment of regular communication channels and rumor control techniques such as the availability of a contact person who can be easily reached with questions and concerns. At one campus they referred to this as the "program review hotline." Another useful rumor control technique is the use of a periodic newsletter providing a progress report or addressing a persistent rumor.

Need for a Coordinator

During this phase of the review process, it is necessary that someone have clear responsibility for seeing that the review effort continues smoothly and on schedule. Usually this responsibility is delegated to a single person—for example, the institutional research officer, an associate dean or associate vice-president for academic affairs, or the program review committee chair at the institutional level. System, district, and state board staff would have this responsibility for reviews at their levels, often associated by institutional coordinators. In these instances, the coordinator of record may be different from those who do the day-to-day coordinating work. In one state the coordinator of record was the vice-president for academic affairs but the actual activities were carried out by the director of institutional research.

The review coordinator is responsible for a number of activities. In addition to working with committees and maintaining communications, typical responsibilities include coordinating site visits and report development by consultants, self-studies of programs being reviewed, and data collection and analysis.

Consultants

If consultants are used in the review, their selection, indoctrination, site visits, and report development must be well coordinated. In a previous chapter we touched on the selection of consultants (that is, experts in the field under review) and noted the importance of engaging persons with certain qualities. Their names can be supplied by a faculty in the program being reviewed, others in the field, professional organizations, learned societies, other institutions, states conducting reviews, and accreditation organizations. If the review is summative in nature, someone outside the program should make the selection and engage the consultants. Typically the number of consultants ranges from one to three or more depending on the program's size and complexity. In Chapter Five we discuss the role of the consultants.

The person responsible for coordinating the consultants should prepare a letter of agreement or contract depending on local procedures. This document should spell out the services expected, the scope of the effort, the specific role of the consultant, the amount of pay or honorarium provided, the extent of out-of-pocket expenses to be reimbursed (enclosing a copy of the local travel expense policy may prevent problems later on), the schedule of the review, the consultant's deadlines, personnel guidelines explaining how the consultant's review is to be handled, the nature of the report expected, the purpose of the review, travel arrangements, data availability to support the site visit, and the person to whom the consultant reports.

The consultant's site visits should include meetings with key persons associated with the program such as faculty, students, administrators, local employers, and graduates. The consultant should also have a chance to review facilities, equipment, and other resources associated with the program. Generally information regarding the program is made available during the site visit, but it may be sent to the consultant in advance. Site visits are not unlike accreditation visits; however, the standards (that is, criteria) of review should be those specifically developed for the program review. The exception to this rule is the situation where the program review and the accreditation review are combined. In this case the accreditation standards should be expanded to include those specifically developed for the program review or vice versa.

It is generally advisable for the coordinator to meet with the consultant upon arrival at the program site. This meeting provides an opportunity to answer questions, introduce the consultant to key persons, reinforce the purpose and scope of the review, orient the consultant to the area, and so on. In some reviews, consultants are free to explore the program at will; in others, the coordinator may accompany them on their rounds. In any case, the coordinator should assist the consultants as needed during the site visit.

Before the consultant leaves the program site, there should be a debriefing in which the general observations and likely conclusions of the visit are conveyed to the program faculty and others such as the coordinator or program review committee. This exit interview presents a unique opportunity for the program faculty (in a formative review) to gain a candid insight into the program. Often matters are discussed by consultants that for reasons of discretion and confidentiality will not appear in their formal report. In one southwestern university, the dean and associate vice-president were advised of some badly needed changes in the faculty. One faculty member was apparently unproductive and needed to be retired, and there were serious gaps in the coverage of the disciplines resulting in the need to provide additional faculty or consider terminating major aspects of the program.

The exit interview is also an opportunity to restate the expectations for the final report. In some places the consultant's payment is withheld until the report has been completed. The consultant's draft report should be reviewed by appropriate persons, including those whose program was reviewed, for factual errors and omissions prior to preparation of the final report. It is not unusual to see draft reports that contain errors and misunderstandings. Failure to correct these problems can result in a loss of credibility not only for the consultant but for the review process itself. The consultant's final report should be sent to the responsible parties (the program faculty in a formative review and the administrator or review committee in a summative review).

Self-Studies

Whether the review is formative or summative, someone needs to supervise the development of the self-study. In a formative review, it is often a person associated with the program such as the department or program chair, but it can also be a faculty member. Sometimes the duties are shared among the faculty in a program, but this is a rare occurrence. In both types of review, a central office, such as an institutional research office, can help in providing data support for the self-study (for example, a set of standardized data for each program being reviewed). In summative reviews, central coordination is more critical to the process because the data collection must be consistent across programs. Regardless of *who* is designated as the coordinator, the key point is that someone at the institution must have overall control of the process.

The tasks of the self-study coordinator typically include the timely collection of information about the program from program faculty, students, alumni, and others. Maintaining a firm schedule is always a challenge, as persons associated with the review frequently have varying levels of commitment to it, creating a need for periodic encouragement to complete their assigned duties.

A complete guide to the preparation and design of the self-study process has been developed by Kells (1983). Kells notes two purposes of self-study that are especially pertinent here: "help institutions and programs improve and to incorporate into the life of the institution a program of ongoing, useful, institutional research and self-analysis" (p. 15). Self-studies can be considered successful to the extent that they achieve these purposes.

Data Collection and Analysis

Data on the program as well as assessment information on students should be collected at a central location and carefully analyzed to ensure that they are accurate and interpreted properly. This generally means that someone with expertise in data collection and analysis as well as persons knowledgeable about the program should have a role in analyzing the data. This expertise will ensure a balanced perspective and accuracy in spotting factual errors and omissions in the data. Failure to review data thoroughly may result in complications later on when decisions are being made about the program. In at least one instance, an institutional review process was derailed due to controversial enrollment data presented with the recommendations to decision makers.

Data analysis is simply the tabulation and interpretation of the raw information collected during the evaluation. The analysis should relate the data to the review's questions, goals, and objectives. Since not all data are relevant to a review, it is necessary to apply analytical expertise to determine their relevance. One of the most frequently noted problems with reviews is data overload: Too many data are collected and not all are capable of assimilation into the review process. This is especially true if data are collected haphazardly because someone thought they would be "good to have" and not because they address the major questions and purposes of the review. If this has occurred, superfluous data must be weeded out. Failure to focus the data can result in an analysis that is technically unsound because it increases the probability of finding significant results by chance alone, because it results in a loss of credibility as the evaluator strays from the plan specifically tailored to answer the evaluation question, and because it is hopelessly inefficient (Ratzlaff, 1986, p. 27).

Some suggest that a pilot test be conducted to find out if the data are relevant. Such a test would include all the planned information analysis activities. This pilot test should reveal whether "the needed information will be available in a manageable form; necessary expert personnel and special equipment such as computers are available; and data reduction procedures are efficient and accurate" (Ratzlaff, 1986, p. 27). This measure may be especially useful in program reviews involving new and complex activities. For the average program review, however, pilot testing may not be needed, but the data's relevance should not be ignored. In some cases the review process reveals new data needs as specific facts must be addressed. These needs should be pursued if they are relevant to the review. At some point, however, the data collection must stop. There are almost always aspects of the review left incomplete due to time and data restraints. Usually these shortcomings do not impede the review.

The data analysis itself brings into play all the statistical and analytic skills of the reviewers. In some cases the questions and purposes of the review are fairly simple and so the statistical techniques are fairly simple. A formative review in which the major evaluation question is whether or not the program is meeting its goals can be answered fairly easily by comparing the focused results of the review with properly stated goals. Either they are being met or they are not. More complex questions in complex programs will require greater statistical and analytic skills. A review that focuses on student outcomes can become a major test of one's analytic ability, especially if one wishes to make management decisions based on the assessment results (Ewell, 1985).

Interpreting the results and developing recommendations can also be a complex task. For example, a program review survey asked whether students used a specific course's information after graduation. The results showed that 40 percent used the course's information. The evaluator has to consider factors that might include the following:

- Is 40 percent sufficient to demonstrate the relevance of the coursework to the program?
- Were the responding graduates representative of all graduates?
- Does a positive response (that is, using the course's information) mean that the program is effective?

These questions deal with different aspects of the analysis. The first concerns standards of merit (how significant is 40 percent?); the second with statistical design (how good was the sample?); and the third with validity of information and analysis (how significant is this question, assuming it was the right question to ask in the first place?).

A common analytic technique in program reviews involves the use of comparative data, either within or between institutions. There are a multitude of data sources that can be used for such comparisons. Christal and Wittstruck (1987) describe some of the available data bases that can be used for this purpose. These comparisons, however, can be quite complex and require special skills to identify accurate data sources and apply these comparisons in meaningful ways. Brinkman (1987) provides a useful guide to data comparisons. He also notes that the fundamental data concerns of validity, accuracy, and reliability apply to comparative as well as other data.

Each question asked in the review and the relevant data must be individually analyzed. The cumulative results of the analysis of all questions are then analyzed to develop an overall sense of the program's effectiveness. This provides valuable information on the program's dynamics and the relationship between parts of the program.

In the final analysis the reliability and validity of the review results must be assessed. Two questions need to be asked: Are the results individually and collectively significant? Are they of programmatic significance?

It is important that the results convey technically adequate information that will allow one to determine the program's worth. In summary, the analysis should:

1. Provide a clear identification of the mission of the program reviewed.
2. Provide sufficient detail about the program so that its likely influences can be discovered.
3. Identify the sources of information so that its adequacy can be assessed.
4. Use valid measurement in its data-gathering instruments and procedures.
5. Use reliable instruments and procedures to ensure that the information is sufficiently reliable for the intended use.
6. Use data control procedures to ensure that the data collected, processed, and reported are correct.
7. Ensure that the data used in the review are appropriately analyzed to result in supportable interpretations.

Summary

Conducting the review itself is the critical phase of the review process. Care must be taken to ensure the proper climate so that support for the reviews is maintained. A key person in this activity is the coordinator, who must supervise the consultants and make sure that data collection and analysis are undertaken in an effective manner.

4

Analyzing, Communicating, and Applying Results

❋❋❋❋❋

All the advantages of a well-designed review and a smoothly executed review process can be lost if the concluding documents are poorly written, if there is a lack of proper involvement, if the results are not properly utilized, and if opportunities for correcting problems identified in the review are not properly handled. In successful reviews, proper care is taken in each of these areas. This chapter offers suggestions for handling the final phase of the review.

Preparing the Report

Most reviews should conclude with a formal written report. If there are groups with different levels of interest involved in the review, it is usually advisable to prepare a report that addresses the specific needs of each group. The preparation of a written report, even if the review is entirely for internal use, is recommended because it allows the reviewers to systematically outline the results of analysis and logically state the outcomes. It also provides the institution a written document of the review.

A typical program review will result in several documents:

- A self-study report prepared by the program under review
- A report by the consultants
- A response to the consultant's report (usually limited to factual errors or omissions)
- A report of the program review committee or person overseeing the report

Each of these documents may be important in its own right, but usually they are summarized in a single document of a size, length, and content appropriate to each group's interest.

Here we will focus on the final report, which is usually designed to consolidate key information in a form useful for the intended audience. But first it is necessary to address some key questions:

1. Who is the intended audience?
   - If there are several audiences, do they need separate reports to address different concerns and levels of expertise?
   - Will oral presentations also be required?
2. Is a formal report required?
   - If so, is a standardized format required?
   - If not, what format would be most effective for the various recipients?
   - What is the specific purpose of the report?
   - How long and detailed a report is needed? Desired? Practical? Is a one- or two-page summary sufficient? Or is a longer report needed?
3. What must the report contain?
   - Will it contain a summary of the review process and involvement?
   - Will it contain recommendations? Is there sufficient information about the program to prepare recommendations? Or is further study needed? Should the recommendations be in a format that facilitates action by decision makers?
   - Is it desirable to make available the full documentation on the review? To only limited audiences?
   - How much will the report cost to produce?

- What will be its distribution? If different reports are to be prepared for different audiences, who will get each report?
- Can the report be prepared quickly?
- If reports will be prepared on a number of programs at the institutional, system, or state levels, is it desirable to have a prescribed or partially prescribed format?

Once these basic questions have been answered, at least tentatively, the preparation of the report can begin. It should go without saying that reports need to be prepared clearly and concisely since they may have significant implications for the program reviewed and even the review process itself. A basic tenet of good communication is that the sender should convey a message in a way that the receiver can best understand it. This may mean, for example, that a report intended for a lay audience (for example, trustees) should keep educational jargon to a minimum and make good use of executive summaries and graphic presentation. The typical review report consists of the following sections, each tailored to the needs of the intended audience:

1. A description of the program reviewed
2. A description of the review process (who, what, where, and when)
3. An analysis of previous review findings and current review results and documents
4. A description of the program's strengths and weaknesses
5. Recommendations and timetable for implementation

Regardless of what format, audience, or mode of presentation is used, the final report should reflect three basic factors: simplicity, clarity, and effectiveness. Responsibility for this task usually falls on one person. Typically the report writer is a chair of the program review committee, a consultant, or a middle-level administrator (and they are not always chosen for the quality of their writing). The person most involved with the review should write the report. To obtain a consensus on the report, it is usually reviewed by others in various stages of development (committee members, other administrators, and consultants) for comment and suggestions. The draft copy of the final report should be shown to the faculty from the program primarily for factual errors and omissions.

Some reviewers suggest that the writer formally pretest the report to get others' reactions before it becomes final. At one college this was done to find out whether one format was better than another for reaching the target audience and to tip the writers off to trouble spots. Such a pretest determines if the report attracts and holds the audience's attention, clearly conveys the main ideas, and is believed and accepted. The pretest report may be shown to key figures or it may be presented in focus group or individual in-depth interviews.

Effective review reports, in addition to being well written and concise, convey a good sense of the program's strengths, weaknesses, and needed action. Often this is achieved by the use of graphics. Graphics have many advantages:

- They create interest and catch the reader's attention.
- They convey visual relationships that can be clearly grasped and easily remembered.
- They are more efficient than words, since the essential meaning of large masses of statistical data can be assimilated at a glance.
- They afford a comprehensive picture of the problem, making for a more thorough and balanced understanding.
- They stimulate analytical thinking and investigation, which brings out hidden facts and relationships (Warmbrod and Persavich, 1981, p. 230).

Here is a checklist that has been found helpful in preparing the final report:

- Could someone totally unfamiliar with the program understand it?
- Are parts of the report redundant?
- Is jargon kept at a minimum?

- Is statistical expertise necessary to understand the report?
- Are recommendations written in a clear and action-oriented manner?
- Are positive solutions listed?
- Are negative findings fairly stated? Are the negative findings stated in a problem-solving rather than a blame-setting context? Have these negative findings been shown to members of the program before being made public? Are the data upon which these recommendations are made defensible? (Warmbrod and Persavich, 1981, p. 241.)

Most final reports will result in little debate, but there are always one or two items that lead to discussion and even controversy. If an outcry is anticipated, special efforts can be taken to communicate the results. A round of program reviews at a midwestern university, for example, resulted in recommendations for several program terminations and reorganizations. When the reports were made public (actually they had been leaked for months), the administration was caught off guard and the resulting publicity was more negative than necessary. A communications expert reviewing this unfortunate outcome recommended that the institution adopt a "crisis communication plan" and avoid three common mistakes:

1. Running things as if the public were not interested. (Nothing stays private for long today.)
2. Straining the bad news as it goes up the chain of command. (Trustees did not know the likely repercussions of the report.)
3. Failing to rehearse spokespersons. (At a news conference, spokespersons said different things leading to unfortunate results.)

An institution in these circumstances may need to activate the crisis team, get the facts, ascertain the damage, stop the bleeding as swiftly as possible, and summon the media and speak candidly about the report and what the institution intends to do with it.

Some institutions and state agencies, where permitted by law, keep certain reports or aspects of reports confidential (for example, the consultant's report). In this way they can control what is made public and minimize the damage to individuals and the institution as a whole. If handled well, with the right people having access to the right information, this approach can work well. If it is not handled well, there may be accusations of "coverups" or "hidden agendas" that could undermine the report's credibility. Such accusations were made at a college that did not allow the program's faculty to see the consultant's report. Other institutions, like the University of Colorado, make all program review reports available to all who want to see them. These institutions feel that openness pays off in dividends supporting the credibility of the review effort.

Using the Results

One of the most devastating results of a review effort is inaction. Faculty, administrators, and others soon lose faith in the review if it is not used in decision making. If the review does not result in a program change, innovation, or improvement, then it has not been used.

Ultimately utilization manifests itself as the review results are incorporated into the planning and budget processes. This does not mean that every recommendation is automatically implemented. If means that every recommendation is given serious consideration and those regarded as feasible and desirable are acted upon. Hence the value of a well-written report and recommendations that get the attention, interest, and support of decision makers.

One way to ensure the results are used is to build the review into a program. This approach is based on the premise that the measurement of a program's implementation need not be separate from program activities. This approach is considered to be more cost-effective, and more useful, because review activities and program activities are integrated so that they are mutually reinforcing and interdependent (Patton,

1988). By integrating the review results in the budget and planning process, the program review is strengthened and the budget and planning process is enhanced. For example, program review has been shown to lead to more effective planning as the strengths and weaknesses of the institution's programs are identified (Barak, 1986).

If the review has not been integrated into the program, other methods must be tried to encourage utilization. Smith (1988) has proposed fifteen ways to facilitate use of the review results:

1. Consider utilization at every evaluation decision point. By the end of the evaluation, the potential for use has been largely determined.
2. Answer the questions that are asked. Credibility involves more than methodological quality; it also involves responsiveness to the specific policy question. Focus data gathering on those factors that are amenable both to manipulation and to intervention with program efforts.
3. Frame findings in terms of the intended users. Findings set in a context of unfamiliar categories and concepts make it difficult for users to translate them into action. Closely related is Weiss and Bucuvalas's (1977) notion of the "conformity of user expectations": The likelihood of users valuing a report increases when the findings agree with their construction of reality.
4. Focus recommendations on incremental rather than comprehensive changes. Small-scale changes are likely to be less disruptive and less likely to meet with resistance.
5. State recommendations as goals rather than delineating specific courses of action. People may be more willing to do something if they can control how it is done.
6. State recommendations in prescriptive terms. Evaluators look back; decision makers look forward. Decision makers want to know what the findings signify for future programming actions.
7. Make sure there is an obvious link between the recommendations and the data. Otherwise the recommenda-

tions may be conceived as ideologically or politically inspired (and therefore mistrusted).

8. Avoid calling into question the organization's beliefs and values.

9. Adhere to rigorous methodological standards of practice. A common strategy of those who oppose report findings is to discredit the methods. Credibility is the "sine qua non of use over the long term" (Chelimsky, 1983, p. 14).

10. Use a combination of approaches to secure information so that the strengths of one can mitigate the weaknesses of another.

11. Time the presentation of findings to the decisions that will be affected.

12. Make findings clear, useful, and available to policymakers. This means ordering them in a policy context, condensing, deleting what is not relevant. Telling all in the same neutral tone can be tantamount to telling nothing. Do not leave it to the policymaker to discern the areas of success. Light and Pillemer (1984) make a similar recommendation about providing policymakers with what is pertinent: "Our policymakers do not lack advice; they are in many respects overwhelmed by it" (p. 17).

13. Rediscover the anecdote. After learning the size of a problem, its range, its frequency, its direction, and its characteristics, one of the most effective ways to present findings in the political forum is to illustrate the general findings via specific cases that focus attention on, or explain, the large points. Anecdotes should not be presented as the only data; they are effective when used in conjunction with the facts and figures.

14. Reduce political barriers. Become thoroughly familiar with the political process, operate within it, recognize the political viability of possible solutions, and know what means are politically acceptable for getting the solutions implemented. Be flexible in dealing with key political players—compromise is the key to achievement. Demonstrate a willingness to consider others' views on matters of mutual interest.

15. Couch findings in the context of other work done in the
     area. Although a survey of the literature is important
     before a study is designed, it is often omitted in the
     interest of time or because evaluative information is mis-
     takenly thought to be for decision makers only. "The
     ability to draw on a large number of soundly designed
     and executed studies adds great strength to the knowl-
     edge base when findings are consistent across different
     studies conducted by different analysts using different
     methods. No single study, no matter how good, can have
     this kind of power" (U.S. General Accounting Office,
     1983, p. 1).

For purposes of decision making, it is helpful to cate-
gorize programs according to the results of the reviews. Here
are four choices one can make as a result of a review:

1. Top programs
2. Good, steady programs
3. Questionable programs
4. Programs to be terminated

It has been our experience that about 10 percent or fewer of
an average institution's programs are considered top programs. These are outstanding programs that are of excellent
quality, that have reasonable costs, and for which there is a
strong demand. Another 50 to 60 percent of an institution's
programs are considered to be good but not outstanding.
These are programs with reasonable costs and good demand
and marketability. They are steady producers that may be
considered the backbone of the institution. About 20 to 30
percent of an institution's programs have problems: inordi-
nately high costs, low demand, questionable quality, and
mediocre marketability. These are the programs that will
require the most attention of decision makers because one
must decide whether the problems are curable or terminal.
With staffing changes, increased funding, and reorganization,
perhaps some of these programs can be turned around and

made into good, steady programs or even top programs. Others may just not be worth the effort. A few of the programs reviewed at a typical institution are so bad that they should be terminated. No amount of resources or effort will make these programs effective. For example, a program may just not attract enough enrollment and faculty to produce a strong program or even a good one.

Some have found it useful to develop a matrix with the programs reviewed on the left margin and the various criteria across the top along with decision categories such as "maintain current resources," "increase resources," and "reduce resources." In addition to these budget categories it might be desirable to have a category for planning decisions across the top, such as "strategic planning action." In this way, programs intended for major focus in the plan can be identified while those not intended for focus can be so designated.

As can be seen in Table 8, Program A is a top program while Program D is a candidate for termination. Program C was chosen for increased resources and planning in order to make it a top or at least a good program. By focusing on Program C, this institution decided to improve the quality of a program that is directly related to the mission of the institution (that is, centrality) and thereby improve its productivity. (Apparently the program had a serious dropout rate resulting in low productivity.) The institution determined that because of its strong market position, it could also increase enrollments.

Perhaps the greatest fear in the review process is the fear of program termination. Discontinuance, however, plays a very small role in most reviews—probably fewer than 5 percent of the programs reviewed at a given institution or statewide review. These programs are more than likely unproductive and inactive "paper programs." They are listed in the catalog and are offered by faculty from another program area that is more productive. Termination of these programs involves little savings.

Melchiori (1982) has indicated several issues that should be kept in mind as one considers the option of program ter-

Table 8. Matrix for Program Review Decision Making.

Program	Cost	Need/Demand	Quality	Centrality	Productivity	Marketability	Recommended Budget/Plan
A	Moderate	Strong	Excellent	Strong	Strong	Strong	Increase/highlight
B	High	Low	Good	Low	Low	Low	Reduce/drop
C	Moderate	Strong	Fair	High	Low	Strong	Increase/redirect
D	Low	Low	Low	Low	Low	Low	Reduce/drop

mination: legal aspects (lack of authority, union contract); interactive issues (decentralized governance); absence of fiscal incentives; political issues; definitional shortcomings (absence of goals and objectives); attitudinal issues (disagreements over values and expectations, burnout of administrators); procedural issues (who is best qualified to review programs); and environmental issues (impact of a specific incident overshadowing all other review efforts).

If, however, it seems desirable to discontinue a program, we strongly recommend that it be done as a result of thorough study. The review itself should provide a solid basis for a decision to terminate a program. If not, a special study may be needed. The plan for discontinuance should seek support from those whose approval matters: the board of trustees, appropriate state agencies, accreditation groups, students, parents, the community, employers, and advisory groups. The plan will detail such activities as the welfare of students (current, past, and potential), enlightened personnel policies for faculty and staff (early retirement, transfers, new job placement), disposition of facilities and equipment, budget adjustments, and public relations.

More likely than program termination are program changes: changes in the program's structure, changes in curricular design, changes in the program's mode of delivery, reduction in budget or staff, elimination of subfields, general phasedown, or various mergers (Melchiori, 1982).

Evaluating the Review Process

In the 1970s, many colleges and universities implemented program reviews as an ongoing systematic evaluation of their academic programs. Much has changed during the 1980s, however. Many colleges and universities have experienced major shifts in funding patterns, clientele, mission, or other strategic decision areas. In addition to these changes, there are other important reasons for wanting to reevaluate an institution's review process. According to a 1982 survey of colleges and universities (Barak, 1982a) these reasons include:

- Obtaining feedback on procedural changes needed to streamline the reviews (that is, efficiency)
- Regaining or strengthening commitment to the review process
- Identifying ways to improve the credibility of the process
- Eliminating uncertainties in the purpose, methodology, and reporting
- Assessing the impact of reviews on academic programs (that is, effectiveness)
- Assessing the impact of the reviews on other decision-making processes of the institution
- Determining whether the cost of the reviews is reasonable and possibly conducting a cost/benefit analysis
- Correcting errors inadvertently built into the review process

Some examples noted by survey respondents illustrate the typical problems encountered with program reviews. In one case it was found that the faculty's "greatest disappointment" was the response (or nonresponse) to the total review effort. Many saw no dividends on the great investment of time. In another effort the evaluators found major problems in the accuracy of the review reports—due in large part to a procedural error that provided no opportunities for timely review of draft reports. Yet another evaluation found serious morale problems due to a different procedural oversight. These examples are but a few of the many problems that can occur in a review process.

The following sections provide a framework for the evaluation of program review processes that can be used by colleges, universities, and higher education agencies to improve their program review activities. We specifically address problems such as those noted above and others we have encountered in our work as consultants to colleges and universities and in national surveys. The approach noted here also builds on the growing literature on program review (for example, Craven, 1980; Wilson, 1984). Our framework is a modified set of the standards developed by the Joint Committee on Standards for Educational Evaluation (1981).

Despite the clear advantages of evaluating the review process itself, only 2 percent of the colleges and universities conducting program reviews in a recent study have conducted a systematic evaluation of their review process (Barak, 1982b). It appears that many program reviewers have failed to grasp the advantages of such an evaluation. As one reviewer noted: "We can hardly muster the interest in doing the reviews; it would be extremely hard to build enthusiasm for evaluating the process of review." Yet there are many benefits to such an undertaking, not the least of which is to gain greater interest in the process.

All the reasons noted above suggest the need for a periodic, systematic evaluation of the total program review process. For the purposes of this book, the term *meta-review* will be used to connote this evaluation. While meta-evaluations have been advocated elsewhere (Stufflebeam and Shinkfield, 1985), here we apply the specific concepts to program reviews in higher education. The next section describes four typical phases and offers suggestions regarding the criteria and the timing of meta-reviews.

Meta-Review Phases

Meta-reviews can be divided into four basic phases: predesign, design, evaluation, and postevaluation. The phases are suggested here as an overall framework for conducting a meta-review. Each phase has a distinctly different focus and a different level of involvement for the various participants. The emphasis placed on each phase depends on the local setting and the evaluation approach that is used. The distinct components of each phase are:

1. Predesign phase:
    *   Identify an initial need for conducting a meta-review.
    *   Identify persons responsible for conducting a needs assessment.
    *   Conduct a needs assessment.
    *   Prepare, review, and accept the needs assessment report.

- Proceed with the next phase if a need is confirmed.
2. Design phase:
   - Appoint someone to conceptualize a meta-review.
   - Consider alternative approaches to the meta-review.
   - Design a meta-review based on the needs assessment.
   - Determine the criteria to be used.
   - Review and accept the design.
3. Evaluation phase:
   - Initiate the evaluation phase.
   - Conduct the meta-review.
4. Postevaluation phase:
   - Analyze the results.
   - Prepare a report of funding recommendations and have it reviewed by key persons.
   - List the activities needed to implement the actions recommended.

Phase 1: Predesign. Ideally the impetus for considering a meta-review is a routine evaluation cycle built into the design of the original program review. This approach is much preferred to the ad hoc use of a meta-review because of some crisis with the reviews. Whatever the purpose, it should be defined so that appropriate mechanisms and activities can be built into the meta-review process. With this purpose in mind, someone who is neutral and open-minded about the program reviews (or a group of appropriate individuals) should be sought. These people will be charged with conducting a needs assessment, or "availability study" as it is sometimes called. The purpose for the needs assessment is to determine the need for the review and then, if appropriate, provide the background work and design effort needed to launch the meta-review.

The needs assessment is a more or less formal effort intended to pave the way for the meta-review by establishing the purpose of the meta-review effort, the results expected as a consequence of the meta-review, the evaluative approach to be used, the resource needs (human and otherwise), and the guiding principles to be used, such as the schedules and the involvement of various constituents (faculty, students, staff, administrators, trustees).

Whether the predesign phase is the sole responsibility of one person or a group of individuals designated formally as a task force or informally as resource persons depends on the local circumstances. The broader the involvement of the various persons with a stake in the reviews, the more likely the ultimate acceptance of the end product. There is no perfect way to organize for the predesign phase except to ensure that those who need to be consulted are appropriately involved (and *perceive* that they are involved).

A number of survey respondents (Barak, 1986) have indicated that timing is an important consideration in conducting a meta-review. When is the best time to conduct a meta-review? Most seem to agree that the two most critical times for a meta-review are at the end of the very first round of reviews (for new processes) and at the end of a complete round of all reviews. If one-fifth of the programs are reviewed each year, for example, meta-reviews are recommended at the end of the very first year (for new review processes) and at the end of five years when all programs have been reviewed.

As a result of the predesign phase, the following issues are usually resolved:

- The need, if any, for a meta-review
- The purpose of the meta-review
- The persons who should be involved in the meta-review and the extent of their involvement
- The general approach that is likely to serve the needs and purposes of the meta-review
- The resources that are likely to be needed (human and otherwise)
- The guidelines controlling the meta-review (that is, deadlines and limitations)

The predesign phase is probably the only phase of the meta-review process that may be optional. If the six elements noted above can be readily determined without a formal needs assessment, it is possible to go directly to the design phase. The primary value of the predesign effort is to provide the groundwork necessary to ensure proper implementation of the meta-review. If this has already been accomplished, there is no need to spend further time and effort in the predesign phase.

Phase 2: Design. The major activity in the design phase is the conceptualization of the meta-review based on the needs assessment (that is, the six items noted above). This is usually assigned, at least initially, to a single person in close consultation with other key figures, although committee designs are not unheard of. Again, in this phase the scale of the effort depends on the complexity expected in the meta-review. The design itself could consist of nothing more than a simple evaluative survey or engaging the services of a knowledgeable consultant. Perhaps the two most difficult aspects of conceptualizing the design are selecting the evaluation approach and selecting the criteria by which the program review process will be judged.

The literature on evaluation contains numerous descriptions of approaches to use in the evaluation of programs. Many of these are theoretical approaches that are not always useful for evaluating a specific program. They are, however, necessary conceptual bases for discussion among evaluation experts. Often the practitioner lacks the time and a working knowledge of evaluation to be able to benefit sufficiently from the often cited models of "true evaluation" (that is, goal-free, goal-based, responsive, decision-making, connoisseurship, and accreditation). For those able and willing to explore such approaches, general descriptions of these models are readily available in Gardner (1977), Popham (1975), and Madaus, Scriven, and Stufflebeam (1983). For those wanting a simpler approach based on a combination of theory and practice in higher education, several examples demonstrating the options are provided in Table 9.

Table 9 represents three typical approaches to meta-review. The chief advantages to the use of outside experts lies

Table 9. Selected Meta-Review Approaches.

Feature	Evaluation by Experts	Self-Evaluation	Combination of Self and Experts
Purpose	To describe, appraise, and suggest ways and means to improve a program review	To foster understanding of review activities and how they are valued in an institution or institutional unit from a variety of perspectives with the aim of improving the process	To describe, appraise, improve, and foster greater acceptability
Typical methods	Expert's expertise and sensitivities	Group discussion, self-study, survey of constituents	Expert's advice and internal discussion and study
Meta-reviewer	Evaluation/program review expert	Institutional faculty and staff	Some combination of reviewer responsibilities involving both experts and critical constituents
Main questions asked	Have the reviews accomplished their purposes? Have other purposes been served? Are there problems with the reviews that need correction? How can the reviews be improved?	What problems and concerns can we identify with our reviews? How can they be improved? Are they cost-efficient? Do they do what we intended? What else do they do?	Combination of questions from other two types

Source: Stufflebeam and Shinkfield (1985); Madaus, Scriven, and Stufflebeam (1983); Kells (1983).

in their presumed neutrality and ability to compare the meta-review with other evaluation processes. Experts are especially beneficial if one is attempting to demonstrate the viability and credibility of the reviews to people outside the institution (trustees, statewide boards, legislators, and others). They can also be helpful if there are sharp divisions within an academic unit or institution and no one is neutral. Even where these conditions do not prevail, it is still important that the meta-review not be a self-serving effort of the persons responsible for the reviews or a hatchet job by those opposed to the reviews. Intellectual honesty and objectivity are as important here as they are in other endeavors. These characteristics should prevail throughout the meta-review process, including the selection of consultants, the use of survey instruments, the analysis and reporting of data, and the writing of the report and recommendations.

Self-evaluations are generally less expensive than consultants and can provide a great degree of participation for those on campus. Various techniques have been used in self-evaluations. One is the discussion method (Kuh and Ransdell, 1980), which has been used for the review of programs and can be adopted for a meta-review. Other successful methodologies include self-studies (Kells, 1983) and survey techniques, which can also be adopted for meta-evaluation. Some combinations of the self-evaluation and expert evaluation techniques, if used properly, have the advantages of both. A fine line needs to be drawn in delineating the respective roles to ensure maximum advantage of the two techniques.

The second most difficult aspect of the design phase is the selection of criteria for the meta-review. This need not be an exhaustive effort, since extensive work has already been undertaken by professional evaluators to develop standards for evaluating activities like program reviews. In 1981 a set of standards for evaluating educational programs was developed and subsequently revised as a result of extensive use in the field (Joint Committee on Standards for Educational Evaluation, 1981). A modified version of these standards applicable to the evaluation of program reviews in higher education is presented in Exhibit 1. These standards have been developed as guiding principles to address the utility, feasibility, accuracy, and ethical aspects of program review.

In addition to these criteria, evaluators should use their own judgment as to what criteria should be used in a meta-review. The decision as to whether or not a given criterion has been met is solely a matter of the evaluator's judgment. Evaluators should be sure to consider the esoteric dimension, both positive and negative, of the review process. This dimension, as one dean described it, "is a reflection upon the dynamic rather than static nature of the review process as it occurs. As in therapy, the review process resembles more than a judicial process, the review procedure changes the attitudes of participants as they go through it. This is true not only within each faculty member's own department, but for the campus as a whole."

After an initial design has been developed, it is usually advisable to obtain consensus on the design as well as to secure the necessary approvals before proceeding. Typical persons consulted at this point include the faculty (at least a sample of those who have been reviewed and otherwise involved in the process); key administrators (including those whose approval is necessary); and administrative staff members who have been involved in the reviews such as institutional researchers and information system coordinators; students and others.

Phase 3: Evaluation. The third phase—the meta-review itself—builds on the efforts of the previous phases. Since the elements of the meta-review depend largely on the evaluative approach selected, it is not possible to offer specific recommendations here. Some general comments, however, may be in order. While obviously this is a critical phase in the meta-review process, there is nothing especially unique about the meta-review that would distinguish it from other evaluative efforts. The process itself needs to be conducted with care to ensure it is fairly done and credible. As in other evaluations, there are those who defend the status quo and those who

**Exhibit 1. Standards for Evaluating
Program Reviews in Higher Education.**

1.0 *Utility Standards*

The Utility Standards are intended to ensure that a review serves the practical information needs of those responsible for the reviews. These standards are:

1.1 *Audience Identification.* Persons involved in or affected by the review should be identified so that their needs can be adequately addressed. Depending on the nature and purpose of the reviews this could include program faculty, administrators, the public, and students.

1.2 *Evaluator Credibility.* The persons conducting the review should be trustworthy, objective, and competent to perform the review so that their findings achieve maximum credibility and acceptance both internally and externally.

1.3 *Information Scope and Selection.* Information collected should be of such breadth and depth and selected in such ways as to address pertinent questions about the programs being reviewed and be responsive to the needs and interests of those with an interest in the program.

1.4 *Valuational Interpretation.* The perspectives, procedures, and rationale used to interpret the findings should be carefully described so that the basis for value judgments is clear and this information is available to the various constituents.

1.5 *Report Clarity.* The program review report should describe clearly the program being reviewed and its context, as well as the purposes, procedures, and findings of the review, so that it will be readily understandable to all what was done, why it was done, what information was obtained, what conclusions were drawn, and what recommendations were made.

1.6 *Report Timeliness.* Release of reports should be timely so that recipients can best use the reported information. If the deadline cannot be met there should be adequate notice of the new deadline. Reports that are delayed repeatedly tend to lose their credibility.

1.7 *Evaluation Impact.* Reviews should be planned and conducted in ways that encourage their use by appropriate persons.

2.0 *Feasibility Standards*

The Feasibility Standards are intended to ensure that a review will be realistic, prudent, diplomatic, and frugal. These standards are:

2.1 *Efficient Procedures.* The review procedures should be efficient so that disruption is kept to a minimum and needed information can be obtained.

2.2 *Political Viability.* The review should be planned and conducted with anticipation of the different positions of various interest groups, so that their cooperation may be obtained and any attempt to curtail review operations or to bias or misapply the results can be averted.

**Exhibit 1. Standards for Evaluating
Program Reviews in Higher Education, Cont'd.**

2.3 *Cost-Effectiveness.* The review should produce information of sufficient value to justify the resources expended.

3.0 *Propriety Standards*
The Propriety Standards are intended to ensure that a review will be conducted legally, ethically, and with due regard for the welfare of those involved, as well as those affected by its results. These standards are:

3.1 *Formal Obligation.* Obligations of the formal parties to a review (what is to be done, how, by whom, and when) should be agreed to in writing, so that these parties are obligated to adhere to all conditions of the agreement or formally to renegotiate it. This is especially true when the review is being conducted by outside contractors.

3.2 *Conflict of Interest.* Conflict of interest, frequently unavoidable, should be dealt with openly and honestly, so that it does not compromise the review process and results.

3.3 *Full and Frank Disclosure.* Oral and written reports on the review should be open, direct, and honest in their disclosure of pertinent findings, including the limitations of the review. They also should be available to anyone with a legitimate purpose.

3.4 *Public's Right to Know.* The formal parties to a review should respect and assure the public's right to know, within the limits of other related principles and statutes, such as those dealing with public safety and the right to privacy.

3.5 *Rights of Human Subjects.* Reviews should be designed and conducted so that the rights and welfare of the human subjects are respected and protected. This includes a concern about the privacy of individual student records.

3.6 *Human Interactions.* Reviewers should respect human dignity and worth in their interactions with other persons associated with a review.

3.7 *Balanced Reporting.* The review should be complete and fair in its presentation of strengths and weaknesses of the program, so that strengths can be built upon and weaknesses addressed.

3.8 *Fiscal Responsibility.* The reviewers' allocation and expenditure of resources should reflect sound accountability procedures and otherwise be prudent and ethically responsible.

4.0 *Accuracy Standards*
The Accuracy Standards are intended to ensure that a review will reveal and convey technically adequate information about the features of the program that determine its worth. The standards are:

4.1 *Object Identification.* The object of the program review should be sufficiently examined, so that the form of the program being considered in the review can be clearly identified.

4.2 *Context Analysis.* The context in which the program exists should

**Exhibit 1. Standards for Evaluating
Program Reviews in Higher Education, Cont'd.**

be examined in sufficient detail that its likely influences can be determined.

4.3 *Described Purposes and Procedures.* The purposes and procedures of the review should be monitored and described in sufficient detail that they can be assessed.

4.4 *Defensible Information Sources.* The sources of information for the review should be described in sufficient detail that the adequacy of the information can be assessed.

4.5 *Valid Measurement.* The information-gathering instruments and procedures used in the review should be chosen and then implemented in ways that will assure that the interpretation arrived at is valid for the given use.

4.6 *Reliable Measurement.* The information-gathering instruments and procedures used in the review should be chosen and then implemented in ways that will assure that the information is sufficiently reliable for the intended use.

4.7 *Systematic Data Control.* The data collected, processed, and reported in the review should be examined and corrected so that the results of the review will not be flawed.

4.8 *Analysis of Quantitative Information.* Quantitative information in the review should be appropriately and systematically analyzed to ensure supportable interpretations.

4.9 *Analysis of Qualitative Information.* Qualitative information in the review should be appropriately and systematically analyzed to ensure supportable interpretations.

4.10 *Justified Conclusions.* The conclusions reached in the review should be explicitly justified so that the audiences can assess them.

4.11 *Objective Reporting.* The review procedures should provide safeguards to protect the findings and reports against distortion by the personal feelings and biases of any party to the review.

---

critize the review effort. All, however, need to feel they are part of the process. Everyone interested should also be kept informed of the progress of the meta-review.

Phase 4: Postevaluation. What happens to the results of the meta-review is at least as important as conducting a fair and credible evaluation. In fact, the ultimate credibility of the meta-review will depend heavily upon the use or misuse of the results. The results of the meta-review need to be analyzed, recommendations proposed, and appropriate actions taken. Following the initial analysis of the meta-review results, it is important to circulate a draft of the report and tentative recommendations to key persons for their comments and suggestions. This group would include those with strong views either pro or con. When these people have had sufficient time to comment (time limits are important), their responses should be taken into consideration in drafting the final report. Responsibility for the final draft should rest with those previously delegated the responsibility. (Some overeager administrators ruin an otherwise credible process by jumping in prematurely at this point.)

Finally, the results of the review should be disseminated to the campus community as a whole or to selected persons. If the meta-review has been conducted in a fair, credible, and systematic way, the effort should result in improved program reviews.

Summary

The program review process should be periodically and systematically evaluated to ascertain if it is meeting the current needs of the institution and to eliminate problems with the reviews. Without such periodic assessments, the program review process may become outdated, inefficient, and of little use to the institution. Even worse, the reviews may be doing great damage to the programs and personnel involved. The solution, therefore, is a systematic meta-review. The meta-review process suggested here should result in program reviews that have greater credibility, efficiency, and effectiveness.

5

Faculty Roles and Institutional Support

✴︎✴︎✴︎✴︎✴︎

Faculty members and institutional staff agree that the most helpful part of the review process is what we learn about ourselves. While this statement is not true for everyone involved in the review process, it applies to faculty and institutional support personnel because of their commitment to the academic programs. Historically, faculty members have been the academy, with the president or head tutor the first among equals. Only in the twentieth century have institutions of higher learning expanded until today they are likely to resemble large corporations in their organizational structure. In the following sections we discuss the role of faculty members and institutional staff in the review process, including the types of involvement faculty members can expect, effective ways for faculty to manage time constraints, and the role of institutional staff in the program review process.

Faculty Roles

In formative reviews faculty members feel the demands of the evaluation especially sharply because they are called upon to prepare large portions of the self-studies, gather data regarding programs and students, meet with consultants, and serve

77

on institutional review committees. In many institutions the faculty member bears the brunt of the workload for the review process but is likely to receive little or no compensation.

Why then do faculty participate in the review process? Most faculty members we interviewed (Breier, 1985; 1986a) answered at first blush, "Because I was told to!" But upon reflection they agreed it is their responsibility since it is they who provide the academic program. Some have compared the faculty role in the review process to doctors in the medical profession who through examinations, boards, and licensing procedures regulate their standards of practice. Others see similarities with the business world where corporations require executives to review production goals and profit margins on a regular basis. Ample evidence and historical precedent have contributed to the belief that program review activities are a faculty prerogative.

Faculty members find themselves called upon to serve in several aspects of program review. In the following pages we describe the four main types of faculty involvement—chairs of review committees, members of review committees, chairs of departments, and members of departments—and the responsibilities and activities involved in each of these roles.

Faculty by virtue of their position in the institutional structure may participate in a variety of ways in program review. The following discussion focuses on the four major ways that faculty may be involved, but keep in mind that faculty members as individuals may have broader roles in an institution.

Chairs of Review Committees. At many colleges and universities, the chief academic officer may appoint a faculty member to act as action officer in the review process. In some cases, the faculty member is given release time and institutional support in the form of secretarial and data processing services to complete the review. The advantage of using faculty members in this role is that they will feel less threatened by the review if it is conducted by one of their own. Furthermore, faculty are especially sensitive to demands on their time and are thus likely to use their time wisely. This role is also consistent with the traditional role of faculty in academic matters.

Chairs of committees are generally given their charge by the chief academic officer and report directly to him or her although some may be appointed by a faculty organization such as the senate or council. Committee chairs may participate in the design of the process, but in some cases they do not exercise any authority over the process. The chief academic officer, with the help of the committee chair, then appoints a review committee to assist with the program reviews. The committee implements the program review process and reports its progress to the chief academic officer.

The chairs of committees buffer the faculty from the demands of the review and basically speak for them in the review process. Care must be taken to select faculty who are highly regarded within the institution and who will be sensitive to political considerations. At an eastern college, for example, the chair quickly sensed that two of the consultants selected by the college's dean were inappropriate for the program review because of their bias against colleges such as the one offering the program. Through a series of meetings with the dean and the committee, the chair worked out an arrangement in which two unbiased consultants were added to the review committee. The resolution turned out to be a win/win situation for all involved, and the review process never missed a beat while maintaining its credibility.

Chairs of committees included in our study (Breier, 1985; 1986a) felt it was beneficial to have faculty in charge of the review process. Participation in the review process created an increased awareness in the overall mission of the institution and the relationship of the various departments to that mission. As one faculty member put it: "The most positive aspect of the program review is that it reinforces the issues of educational programs and increases the perceptions of the people surrounding the program so that the program can be reinforced and enhanced."

Chairs of committees gained an appreciation for the

complexity of administration and believed that program reviews improved communication between faculty and administration. They said the use of faculty as chairs was both cost-effective and efficient and an extension of the faculty's governance role. The disadvantage cited by most faculty was lack of resources, both clerical and data processing, to do a first-rate review. These concerns are discussed later in this section.

Members of Committees. Faculty members are often asked to serve as members of review committees and task forces or as evaluators for other programs. Such participation in the review process is usually beneficial to all concerned but requires time, commitment, and a depth of understanding of the review process in order to achieve an excellent review.

Most faculty members have had some experience with peer review or evaluation through the regional and specialized accrediting processes. While this experience can be useful to the program review, the two processes are dissimilar. Nevertheless, faculty will have observed the accreditation process as it occurs in their programs and on campus. Newcomers to program review should acquaint themselves with the process by discussing the accreditation process with their dean or chief academic officer. Key questions to ask are: How do you determine the validity of the self-study? What kinds of data should I expect to see? How do I ask to see data not presented? Who determines the priorities of the review? Familiarization with these details enables faculty to bridge from the known process of accreditation to the unknown process of program review.

As members of a review committee, faculty may be asked to review programs within their institution. If they are asked to evaluate programs at other institutions, they are then considered peer consultants. For our purposes, we will restrict our discussion to program reviews conducted within the institution, although some of the same points apply to faculty acting as consultants.

In most cases faculty are chosen to serve because they are respected by their peers, are considered objective, and have demonstrated good judgment in their personal relations. On some campuses, every program has a review committee and all faculty are expected to serve whenever their committee is involved in a review. In this case, the program review process has already been designed and the committee is responsible for implementing it. A more prevalent method is to select a review committee for each program as it is needed. In this case, the review committee designs the process as well.

In either case, care is taken to choose committees that represent a balance of backgrounds, disciplines, and personality. Committees should have representatives from the major disciplines on campus such as the sciences, liberal arts, and professional programs, from the faculty ranks ranging from assistant to full professor, from males and females, and from ethnic groups. Faculty members serving on the committee should understand that they are representatives of the institution as a whole as well as individuals and should be sensitive to the issues that affect their peers. A professor with a strong background in qualitative methodology, for example, was chosen to serve on a review committee in the physical sciences. This faculty member was highly skilled in interviewing and through a series of interviews with faculty, students, and alumni was able to discern problems not readily visible in the self-study. Because of his background in methodology, the organization and presentation of his final report persuaded the dean and the academic vice-president that changes were needed in the science programs.

Faculty members serving on the review committee should expect leadership from the chairs of the committees: consulting with faculty members about acceptable meeting times, providing copies of review materials with ample time for study, preparing and distributing agendas, and consulting with committee members about key issues. A faculty member involved in a review has the right to expect such activities and should request them in the initial meeting with the department chair. In return faculty are obligated to review the material carefully, to attend all scheduled meetings, to participate fully in discussions, and to help write the final report.

Faculty indicate that they devote about 20 percent of their time to the review process and are able to conduct the reviews without sacrificing other duties. The time commitment will vary from process to process. If review activities are scheduled in advance, adjustments are easier and faculty can withdraw from other campus activities to accommodate the review schedule. If the schedule is not prepared in advance, faculty may have to make hasty adjustments to already crowded schedules. They may be able to change other committee assignments or ask for a temporary leave from an assignment during the review activities. Other possibilities include requesting additional student assistants for clerical and grading purposes and suspending research activities. Unless some changes are made in the schedule, faculty members given short notice will find it hard to participate fully in the review.

As the process unfolds, faculty are provided various reports and data prepared by the program under review. The material may consist of a self-study in narrative form, a series of tables or charts illustrating different types of data, or answers to the committee's questions. This material is regarded as an early step in the review process, and additional information may be required.

The second step typically consists of visits or interviews with faculty, staff, and students of the program under review. The visits may be made by the review committee as a whole, or each member of the committee may be asked to visit certain individuals. Obviously the first approach allows everyone to have an in-depth experience of the program, a shared experience, while the second approach requires additional committee time for members to report the results of their visits. The type of approach used by the committee is a matter of discussion and should be decided in the initial meetings.

Once the committee has reviewed all the relevant data and met with the key people in the department, the committee members should be given time to consider the information. The committee should meet to determine the type of report it wishes to prepare, who will answer the various parts of the report, and when the report is due. Committee members may write the report collectively, but usually, for the sake of time, individual members write different sections, which the committee as a whole edits into a final report. Faculty members should keep a copy of the report with their notes on the review process for future use. Such files are useful in preparing dossiers for promotion and tenure, for faculty evaluation reports, and for refreshing memories prior to another review.

Faculty members who serve on review committees express concern about managing their time, maintaining objectivity, and becoming involved in departmental or interdepartmental conflicts. The best way to handle such concerns is to have a sound review process in place with agreed-upon evaluation criteria and to conduct the review in a businesslike manner. These concerns should be discussed fully and openly with the chair of the review committee in the initial meetings.

Chairs of Departments. Many institutions assign major review responsibilities to chairs of departments. These responsibilities can include overall coordination of the self-study, selecting possible consultants (though usually not the final choice), maintaining faculty morale in the face of the added workload of the review, verifying and, in some instances, collecting data, and explaining the program to consultants or other reviewers. So important are these key functions that failure to perform them well can result in a poor-quality review. Except for data collection, these functions cannot really be delegated elsewhere in the institution.

Most department chairs have responsibility for preparing the self-study, but frequently they rely on faculty members within the department to prepare various sections of the report. A typical arrangement is to have faculty members write a description of their program areas. The department chair may ask them to compile some statistics regarding enrollments, course offerings, program requirements, attrition and graduation rates, and the success of graduates in their fields if such data are not readily available. Faculty members are also asked to update their résumés, which are placed on file in the department office or included as an appendix to the self-study.

Once the various department members have prepared their sections of the self-study, the department chair edits them into a unified report. Occasionally faculty members revise certain sections or expand on key points, but generally the editing is done by the department chair. This task alone consumes a great deal of time. Department chairs report that approximately 15 percent of their weekly time is devoted to compiling and editing reports during the review process plus additional time for departmental meetings.

Department chairs must be careful not to portray too bleak a picture of their department in the self-study. Faculty can become divided over this issue. Some may feel the department is underfunded and wish to paint the darkest picture possible; others may fear that too much pessimism might cause the department to be reduced or eliminated. In a southwestern college that was undergoing a statewide program review, the faculty wanted to emphasize the effects of underfunding in the self-study. The department chair, however, was concerned about reprisals: "I was reluctant to paint so bleak a picture for fear the board would say if you are so underfunded you may not need the program or department and move to eliminate it." In this case the dean's office supported the department chair, and the report was revised to reflect a more moderate view. Department chairs need to understand the purpose of the review and to depict accurately the status of their department as it compares to other departments in the institution and at peer institutions. When in doubt about the appropriate course, it is a wise department chair who consults with key figures regarding the final version of the self-study.

Another important consideration for department chairs is the selection of consultants. The department may be asked to forward several names of consultants they desire to review their program. In discussion with the faculty, department chairs should look for consultants with a reputation for fairness and thoroughness, familiarity with the program and institution in question, and a degree of objectivity. Occasionally former faculty members who have moved to other institutions may be asked to serve as review consultants. In some cases this is acceptable, but in many cases objectivity is compromised and the department does not get the balanced review it deserves.

Sometimes faculty morale deteriorates during the review process due to increased workloads and the pressure of deadlines and schedules. Department chairs who are sensitive to this concern can work in advance to reduce the demands on faculty. Some department chairs write most of the self-study themselves and circulate a draft copy for faculty to correct or edit. Others arrange for additional clerical and secretarial support for the faculty involved in the review. Student assistants can be employed to work with faculty in data collection, photocopying, and general clerical duties. Ideally the department chair should schedule the department meetings in advance with ample notice, adhere to a printed agenda, limit discussion to matters at hand, and prepare minutes that serve as records of proceedings. Above all, department chairs should keep the faculty fully informed of all steps of the process and give recognition, both verbally and in writing, for jobs well done. We were surprised to learn in our study that department chairs rarely thought to write a letter of appreciation to faculty for serving on a review committee.

The next step occurs when the consultants come to campus. A schedule of the visit should be prepared in advance and cleared with the appropriate persons. Faculty, students, and staff should be notified of the timetable, rooms reserved, and any extra materials or displays prepared. If additional information has come to light since the preparation of the self-study, a short summary should be prepared. The department chair should expect to spend several hours with the review committee answering basic questions about the department, faculty, and programs and then to see that the consultants or the review committee meet with selected faculty, staff, and students. Sometimes review committees specify in advance who they want to see; at other times, they leave the agenda to the department chair's discretion. It is important, though, that consultants visit people who represent the department in terms of programs, personalities, and problems. The chair can play an important role in this effort.

The department chairs in our study expressed several concerns: problems associated with additional workloads on the faculty and support staff; lack of a departmental role in data identification and verification; lack of guidelines (or ambiguous guidelines) for the self-study; the absence of resource support for typing, copying, and consulting; the absence of consistent and comparable information on other units on the campus; and the misuse of consultants. The most frequent concern was failure to use the review results (Breier, 1985; 1986a). While some of the academic vice-presidents and deans seem never to forget the review results, many neglected to use it for any discernible purpose.

Members of Departments. At some point in their career most faculty members are likely to be involved in a program review, at least as a member of a program under review. What responsibilities does this entail? The faculty member will probably learn of the impending review from colleagues or in a departmental meeting. As soon as the review process is established, the department chair should hold a departmental meeting to state the facts and outline a procedure. It is important at this time for the faculty member to ask questions to ensure that the process is fully understood.

Faculty members may be asked to prepare certain sections of the self-study in which they have specialized knowledge and expertise. The department will then review all the sections and edit them into a final report. All parties must take their involvement in the process seriously to assure that individual programs and specialties as well as other department programs are represented fairly and that the self-study reflects a balanced and accurate picture of the department. The department will be judged on the content of the self-study as much as any other aspect of the review.

Once the self-study is completed, most faculty members

will have limited involvement with a summative review until the final report is issued. In most reviews, faculty are asked to meet with the consultants when they are on campus. Faculty members should remember the need for accuracy and openness and provide the consultants with a fair and honest answer to their questions. The amount of time a faculty member may spend on these activities ranges from 5 to 10 percent of a work week for a period of several months. When added to already crowded schedules and the normal anxiety that accompanies a program review, these additional responsibilities can create morale problems. The following checklist suggests ways in which faculty members can manage their time wisely and thus reduce stress:

- Ask for clearly defined criteria for evaluating the program early in the review process.
- Define secretarial and clerical responsibilities for gathering data and preparing reports.
- Discuss the relationship between serving on the committee and promotion and tenure.
- Keep track of time spent in review activities to present for periodic evaluations.
- Try to minimize time spent in meetings and discussions by requesting an agenda and minutes.
- Prepare a memorandum of record at the conclusion of the review detailing your thoughts and feelings about the process and any suggestions you have for future reviews. Show the memo to your department chair or those responsible for the review at the appropriate time. This will assist them in evaluating the review process.

Institutional Staff

Most program reviews involve two levels of institutional staff and a number of departments and offices. The support persons of these offices provide critical assistance and may, in some cases, design and conduct much of the review themselves. It is important to understand the different levels of staff participants and recognize their contribution to the program review process. Institutional staff are defined here as people who work in academically related offices and whose duties generally include planning and managing specific tasks. The two levels of support personnel discussed in this section are the school or department staff and the institutional staff, which includes the academic affairs office and the institutional research office.

In formative reviews, faculty frequently conduct the majority of the review, but involving the institutional staff will improve the quality of the review. These personnel are familiar with other types of institutional data, have easy access to external contacts and resources, and are frequently more knowledgeable than faculty about the institutional setting. In summative reviews, regardless of the level or type of staff involvement, the functions are similar. Typical duties of institutional staff are:

• Coordinating the program review and keeping all interested parties informed of its progress. They may act individually or as members of a review committee.
• Coordinating the data collection portion of the program review and ensuring that the data are correctly analyzed and interpreted.
• Supervising the preparation of any documents, self-studies, or reports associated with the program review.
• Scheduling consultants' visits, coordinating the timetable of the process, and making all the arrangements for meetings, visits, or conferences associated with the program review.

The involvement of the various levels of institutional staff often depends on the size of the institution. Large research-oriented institutions have large staffs with differentiated functions and several different levels. Small liberal arts colleges and community colleges often operate with a smaller staff and resources. The differences between these types of institutions are discussed further in the following paragraphs.

In a formative review, the unit may not need much support from institutional staff, but they should be aware that this support is frequently available and can be supplied if needed. In a summative review, the support is often utilized. In the following sections we describe the functions and roles of the two general types of support typically found in a summative program review.

School or Departmental Support. The first type of support influencing the program review process is found at the college, school, or department level, depending on the size of the institution and how it is organized. In large institutions where several departments are organized into schools or colleges, the dean's office may have several persons who can assist with program review. While their primary responsibility may be in other areas (budgeting, development, public relations, advising), they may be asked to assist with the program review. These people are generally associate or assistant deans or administrative assistants with specialized technical knowledge regarding individual programs (as is often the case in professional programs) or program review. Associate and assistant deans have a great deal of experience with a particular unit and have often participated in numerous reviews. Their contributions are valuable and provide insights often overlooked by others. They derive their influence from thorough knowledge of the programs, the units, and the institution. Administrative assistants may have worked their way up from entry-level positions of secretary or clerk, or they may be graduate students aspiring to be future administrators. They derive their influence from their relationship to the dean and often control the flow of information into the dean's office.

In smaller institutions, a faculty member can be given release time to conduct the program review and write the necessary studies. In this case the support personnel work only temporarily on the program review and return to their full-time faculty duties at the end of the review cycle. This pattern has been followed less often in recent years as institutions adopt a policy of continuous program review.

The role of college, school, or departmental support personnel will, of course, vary according to the institution and the program review's design, but some common duties are evident. Support personnel assist the department chairs in gathering data for the report and in securing special reports from the institutional research office. These people also serve as a link between the departments and the dean and should keep the dean informed of any developments in the program review process that may adversely affect the school or college's position within the university. Staff members see that units or programs adhere to the timetable and review the reports that come into the dean's office. Departmental support personnel should have a good rapport with the unit or program heads and faculty so that questions regarding the reports can be handled informally and without criticism.

Occasionally, it is necessary for a support person to write or rewrite major portions of a self-study. Sometimes the program chairs are so burdened with other administrative and teaching duties that they are unable to devote the time necessary to preparing the report. Or it may happen that the report is not written in the proper style or format. Although evaluating academic programs is usually considered to be a faculty prerogative, preparation of the final report is sometimes delegated to a support person to conserve time for the faculty. This practice should not be encouraged. If the review is to be meaningful, the appropriate faculty and unit heads must stay involved throughout the process.

Institutional Support. Institutional support may consist of several different offices or areas of responsibility, depending on how the program review process is designed. Large research-oriented institutions typically divide responsibility for the program review between several offices. The design and implementation of the program review is often coordinated with the academic affairs office while the data gathering is performed by the institutional research office or its equivalent. Each of these offices may have staff to assist with the program review. Within the academic affairs office, the chief academic officer normally has final responsibility for the conduct and outcome of the review. Certain aspects of the review may be delegated to administrative assistants, specialists, and committees, or to the various academic schools or colleges, but the chief academic officer usually retains control over the general process. In some institutions, the graduate dean has responsibility for the program review because program reviews used to be done primarily for graduate programs. As the program review process has expanded to include all academic programs, responsibility for the review has gradually shifted to the chief academic officer.

The institutional research office works closely with the chief academic officer in preparing data to support the review. Normally the director of institutional research meets periodically with the chief academic officer to review the data requirements. The director then delegates different tasks to various members of the support staff. For instance, one institutional research person may be assigned the task of providing all the academic units with the data on student credit-hour production while another member may be responsible for doing the alumni follow-up studies. Careful coordination and close communication are necessary between the different staffs to ensure the review is successful.

Most smaller, specialized institutions operate with a limited support staff. This point is a strength from the standpoint of reducing communication and coordination concerns, but it puts the burden of conducting the review process on one or two people. Again the chief academic officers often have the major responsibility for the review, but they have only limited assistance from the institutional research office or other support personnel. In one college the chief academic officer relied on the registrar's office to provide the necessary data for student credit-hour production, enrollment trends, and course history. This process was laborious and obliged the vice-president to perform calculations and comparisons between schools or departments without computer assistance. In another small institution, the institutional research function was provided by a faculty member given release time, which meant that the data had to be limited to the bare essentials of current enrollment. In another college, the chief academic officer was assisted by a planning committee consisting of both administration and faculty. In this institution, the data gathering and analysis were done by the members of the committee. As demonstrated by these examples, there are a variety of ways for a small college to conduct a program review. Each institution must assess its resources and plan a process that will work within the institutional framework.

The role of institutional support staff varies from limited involvement to almost total control over the program review process. Their position is pivotal, for the outcome of the review process may hinge on their involvement in the review and how it is perceived on campus. During a formative review, they assist the unit under review by answering questions, providing data where appropriate, and helping to assess the program's outcomes and goals.

In a summative review, the institutional support staff is usually the liaison between the department and the authority requesting the review. It is their responsibility to distribute all the forms that will have to be completed and, in some cases, design the forms themselves. They should be able to define all the terms, explain the criteria being used, and specify the types of data the department must provide in order to respond to the program review. If the process is not well designed, problems can result. One institutional researcher, unaware of what types of data most academic departments can provide, devised a complicated statistical model requiring faculty and department heads to analyze the cost of various programs. The result was a program review that was sharply criticized by faculty and useless to chief administrators.

As the program review develops, the institutional research office becomes an important resource. This office can produce the data that are needed to respond to the program review criteria: student credit-hour production, headcounts per program, faculty loads per department, student-faculty ratios, and employability of graduates. The institutional research office may be able to furnish the data as a matter of routine reporting. In other cases, the office will have to write special computer programs to generate the data. To facilitate the program review process, the institutional research office should be apprised of the anticipated data needs and should be kept continually informed of any changes in these requirements.

Questions regarding the types of information requested should be answered as quickly as possible. The support personnel may have to negotiate the data requirements with the various units undergoing the reviews in order to ensure that standard definitions are applied throughout the review. The support personnel must know in what form the data are available and can often influence the design of the review by negotiating the data requirements to fit the reporting formats of the institution.

Another function of institutional support personnel may be to summarize the data and self-studies that are submitted by the departmental units. In doing this, the support personnel should be aware of the departmental mission and its relationship to the other departments on campus. Certain departments may have special course requirements or teaching loads that may skew some data elements. Music faculty often teach private lessons that may apply toward their teaching load, for example, and nursing programs may count clinical experience as part of the teaching load. The staff person should carefully analyze the self-studies, discuss any questions with the program or unit under review, and ask for revisions if reports are ambiguous or unclear. Only after the report is thoroughly understood should the support personnel begin the analysis and summary process. If at all possible, one person should summarize all the program or unit reports in order to ensure clarity and maintain a common format and style.

Summary

Faculty and institutional staff play an important role in the program review process by providing basic data for the self-study and by serving on the review committee. Faculty can become involved as chairs of review committees, members of review committees, department chairs, and members of departments. Faculty members are seldom given substantive rewards, but research indicates that they take their review responsibilities seriously.

Support personnel are involved in the program review process either at the school or department level or at the institutional level, which includes the academic affairs office and the institutional research office. While the extent of their involvement depends on the size of the institution, support personnel assist with design and implementation of the review, data gathering and analysis, and preparation of the reports. The involvement of institutional staff can do much to ensure a successful program review.

6

Roles of Administrators, Trustees, and State-Level Staff

❊❊❊❊❊

The program review process concerns not only the faculty and staff who deliver the academic programs within an institution but also the people who have general responsibility for the policies of higher education such as administrators, governing boards, and legislators. This chapter examines the role of these figures in the review process and explains how they can assist in the implementation of a successful program review.

College Administrators

College administrators have pivotal roles in the organizational structure of universities. As boundary spanners they interpret the academic environment and mediate differences between internal constituents, such as faculty, students, staff, and boards of trustees, and external constituents such as parents, accrediting agencies, coordinating or state boards, legislators, and the community. Aldrich and Herker (1977) describe two basic functions performed by boundary spanners: information processing and external representation. "Information from external sources comes into an organization through boundary roles, and boundary roles link organizational structure to environmental elements, whether by buffering, moderating, or influencing the environment. Any given role can serve either or both functions" (p. 218).

The typical college or university is organized into four divisions: academic, advancement, finances, and student services. The president is the chief spokesperson for the institution. The administrators in each of these divisions have a boundary-spanning role by linking the faculty and students within the institution with the external public. They assess and disseminate information about the public to the faculty and students and report information about the institution back to the public. In this way they influence the flow of information between the institution and the public and buffer the college from external pressures.

The boundary-spanning operation occurs on a daily basis in numerous ways and is so routine that most administrators do not even note their interactions with the external public. Examples of this activity include the business community approaching the chief academic officer about a new degree program, a potential donor alerting the advancement officer about a scholarship she wishes to endow, or members of the community expressing concern about an apparent increase in drug-related activity among college students and discussing the issue with the student services administrators. All of these examples are part of the boundary-spanning process in which administrators and the public exchange information.

The boundary-spanning role is clearly evident in program review as administrators at various levels interpret, shape, and respond to the demands of the process. In a summative review, administrators work to ensure that the process has credibility and usefulness to the various constituents. The president may delegate the review responsibility, for instance, to the chief academic officer, an institutional research office, or a committee, but maintains final responsibility for the overall effort.

In a formative review, administrators serve as counselors or facilitators and the results of the review have a more focused application. A department may, for example, after conducting a program review, decide it needs to alter its program requirements and offer new courses. One traditional home economics department in a four-year college completed a program review and decided that it should change its approach from traditional courses in foods and textiles to a more relevant emphasis on family nutrition and parenting skills. Such results would be of interest to students, faculty, and administrators but would probably be of little interest to those outside the institution. In a small private liberal arts college, a traditional English department curriculum was altered after a program review and began requiring courses in Eastern as well as Western literature. This change involved considerable discussion with faculty outside the department, the alumni, and benefactors of the college.

In their role as boundary spanners, administrators are expected to explain the needs of the institution to outside constituents while interpreting the external forces to the students and faculty. We have found that during the program review process, almost every level of administration from president to department chair performs some boundary-spanning duties. This is especially true in summative reviews. Through these actions administrators manage the program review process and, to some degree, the responses to it. The more skillful the administration is at interpreting the external environment and providing the appropriate responses to it, the greater the administrative power in the program review process. "The organization thus relies upon the expertise and discretion of its boundary role personnel. They have gatekeeper's power, and may become even more powerful if they make correct inferences and if the information is vital for organizational survival" (Aldrich and Herker, 1977, p. 227).

In the following sections we describe the types of administrative involvement in a program review, offer insights into effective "gatekeeping," and present examples of activities that administrators, governing boards, and legislators frequently undertake in a program review. By administrators we mean presidents, chief academic officers, deans, directors, and review committee chairs who participate in a program review. Departmental chairpersons are, for the purposes of this study, considered faculty and are discussed in Chapter Five.

Since organizational structures vary widely in higher education, the following discussion of administrative participation is generalized. Regardless of the organizational structure, keep in mind that at most levels administrators perform some gatekeeping functions in the program review process, and frequently the review's success hinges on the performance of key administrators.

Presidents or Chief Executive Officers. At the top of the organizational structure, the president or chief executive officer (CEO) has the ultimate responsibility for the program review. As in all decisions in an institution, it is the CEO that the governing body holds responsible. If an institution fails to gain regional accreditation, for example, the board will hold the CEO responsible, not the self-study committee. This principle holds true in program reviews as well, and while most program reviews are conducted by faculty and lower-level administrators, the CEO accepts full responsibility for the process and its outcomes. When a poorly designed and implemented review process resulted in considerable controversy over the proposed elimination of a program, a community college board fired the college president and ordered a suspension of program review activities.

In interviews with CEOs at various institutions, all of them recognized this responsibility and accepted it. As one chancellor stated, "my role is to work with the academic vice-president and other vice-chancellors to ensure that all reviews were properly prepared and all responses to the reviews were answered appropriately." The involvement of system or state-wide CEOs is similar to that of institutional CEOs. The CEOs recognize that the program review process must be credible to the public; their major function in the process is to certify to the various constituents (governing boards, legislators, alumni) that the institution has developed and implemented an appropriate and trustworthy process. In order to accomplish this, CEOs delegate the design and implementation of the program review to their chief academic officers, consultants, and committees.

Program reviews are time-consuming, and CEOs simply do not have the time to be involved on a daily basis with program review activities. They should, however, be knowledgeable about the process and be able to discuss its ramifications with outside constituents. Above all, the CEO should support the process. Program reviews, particularly summative ones, are highly political in nature. As decisions regarding the fate of an academic program are weighed, political pressure will be exerted on the CEO, who must be prepared to protect the process from political action. It is virtually impossible to insulate an institution from political pressures, but if the faculty and students perceive that the program review is being governed by political considerations, the credibility of the process will be irrevocably damaged. Therefore, the primary gatekeeping function of the CEO in the program review process is one of buffering the institution from outside pressures. The president of a state university in Kansas expressed this view when he noted that the program review reaffirmed the institution's commitment to teacher education. Before the program review, the institution had been attempting to be all things to all people. Through the program review process, it defined teacher education as its central mission and was able to convert those who favored other educational programs to the teacher education mission.

The CEOs we interviewed felt that the program review process was a positive one that allowed their institution to improve the quality of its programs while educating the public with regard to institutional strengths and weaknesses. Program reviews help CEOs to ensure accountability, and most of them use the outcomes of the process as a measure of the institution's quality. The president of a four-year public institution said: "It is healthy for institutions to look at themselves, and it is valuable to have outside consultants brought in. They provide more data. It makes the institutions focus on the departments and make decisions about the departments."

When asked what they would recommend to other CEOs about the program review process, most said that the institution needed more time to do an adequate job of reviewing their academic programs. Sensitive to the pressures on faculty and staff, CEOs felt that most reviews burdened faculty and wished they could find ways to relieve some of those burdens. Changing the scheduling of reviews and the length of review cycles were mentioned as possibilities, but most CEOs felt that the results of most program reviews justified the amount of time devoted to them.

Chief Academic Officers. In most institutions, the major responsibility for the program review rests with the chief academic officer (CAO). It is their responsibility to start the ball rolling and see that the process flows smoothly. In every institution we studied, the CAO either participated in the design of the process or, in the case of state-level reviews, made significant contributions to the process and coordinated the campus approach to the review.

The CAO's role in the program review depends on his or her administrative style. One approach is the decentralized process, which assigns responsibility to individual academic units (departments, divisions, or schools) and allows them to develop their own approach. In some instances, the CAO's staff would coordinate data gathering; in other cases each academic unit was responsible for its own data gathering. At one private liberal arts college in Texas, the CAO used the accumulation of data itself as a measure of the department's quality. He noted that he chose not to provide the data to the departments because it was their responsibility to keep it themselves—and, furthermore, "those that kept good data survived, and those that didn't died." Another approach, frequently found in smaller institutions, is the centralized process. In this instance the CAO gives general guidance, may actually chair the review committee, and specifies the areas to be reviewed, the criteria, and the process. The advantage to the centralized approach is that it conserves the faculty's time and energy, produces a uniform outcome, and establishes a standard by which all programs are compared.

The CAO performs a vital function by interpreting the process and guiding the faculty during its implementation. One CAO explained that his role was "to intellectualize" the campus about the process through leadership channels. Such channels might include the faculty governance structure, student governance, alumni groups, governing boards, and community advisory groups. When appropriate, it is the CAO's job to provide the research base and rationale for the process, obtain results from other institutions, and warn against possible pitfalls that the campus should avoid.

When asked what advice they would give regarding program reviews, CAOs had several suggestions. First, they agreed that the process was often burdensome to faculty and that faculty should be given rewards or recognition for participating in the review. Some institutions provided release time to faculty who served on review committees; some regarded service on a review committee as evidence of the institution's support for promotion and tenure; a few simply made it a point to publicly thank faculty and write letters of appreciation. Some CAOs emphasized the need to prepare faculty members for their participation in the review process: "They have got to understand that they get exposed to the good, the bad, and the ugly." This preparation could include providing frequent opportunities for faculty participation in governance, attendance at program review workshops and conferences, acquainting them with resource materials such as this handbook, and connecting faculty with programs at other institutions that have conducted program reviews.

Finally, CAOs warn about the political nature of program reviews. The administration loses credibility when the process does not show results. Institutions should be realistic about the purpose of program reviews and the results that they yield. The process will not diffuse political pressure, and it will not make tough decisions regarding academic programs. It will only yield information on the various programs. It is still up to the administrators to decide how to use the reviews, including the allocation of resources. Chief academic officers should not regard the program review as a means of escaping political pressure. In fact, the political environment is so pervasive that one ought to expect its influence to be felt every step of the way in such a process.

Deans of Schools or Colleges. Within the program review process, it is often the dean's responsibility to ensure that the data on the academic program are accurate, reflect the nature of the program, and provide a fair and balanced view of the program. Unlike faculty whose knowledge is generally limited to one or two program areas, most deans have a breadth and depth of knowledge about a variety of academic programs and can evaluate their strengths and weaknesses. Therefore, they can oversee the program review process so that it truly describes the academic programs under their control. To be thorough in our treatment of the program review process, we will divide the discussion into the role of deans and the role of associate or assistant deans.

Deans often take an active role in the program review, appoint faculty to review committees, and may charge the committees and monitor the data gathering. At the University of Florida, the dean of one school had a graduate assistant whose sole responsibility was to prepare the fact book for the program reviews. He felt strongly that the success of a program review depends on a good data base and took responsibility for the data himself.

Because deans are not often involved in the design of the review process, they expressed frustration over the interpretation of the criteria and methods outlined for data collection. Problems arise over operational definitions of various criteria: how to count faculty who teach in more than one program, how to handle areas of concentration that are not academic programs, and how to differentiate various types of research. Deans need to maintain communication with those responsible for coordinating the review in order to work out acceptable definitions and interpretations of such questions.

In our experience deans are far more negative about the program review process than either the chief academic officer or the chief executive officer. One dean commented, "I was surprised about the lack of sensitivity and understanding by [those in charge of the review] and about the time needed to prepare the reports and data. This review exemplifies what happens when you don't have time to do a good job. I felt the program review was shallow, lacked substance, showed inadequate review of the institutional reports, lacked a sense of direction and cohesiveness, and was fragmented." Such feelings may result from frustration over the data gathering portion of the process; they may also relate to the gatekeeping function. One dean of a large university in the southwest noted that he had almost no role in a review process that was operated out of the academic vice-president's office. While he had access to the review results, he had no say in the initiation of the reviews or in the utilization of the results. He also wanted an opportunity to meet with the consultants before the reviews to explain the mission of the college and the specific role of the program under review in order to prevent unrealistic recommendations.

In the daily operations of an institution, deans, especially in large centralized universities, normally have substantial power over the decisions affecting their academic programs. That is, they hire and evaluate faculty and staff, allocate resources, and influence virtually every area of the academic environment. During the program review, that power is often diminished because control over the process is in the hands of the chief academic officer, a review committee, or consultants at one extreme or the faculty at the other.

Deans accustomed to performing a vital gatekeeping function of influencing the environment find their influence greatly diminished and, therefore, express frustration with the process. Good communication between the deans and those responsible for the program review could alleviate much of this concern. A good example of how personal initiative can influence the process was demonstrated in one college. In this review process the dean's role was poorly defined, but the dean chose to exercise a great deal of influence by personally reviewing and approving the data collection instruments. She also had a major say in selecting consultants and implementing the review results. Without the exercise of personal initiative, this dean might not have had such an important role in the review process.

The deans we interviewed had several suggestions for others in similar positions. First, they recommended that all deans begin building a good data base on their academic programs regardless of whether they were being reviewed or not. Good data bases include longitudinal data on program graduates, which require several years to accumulate. Most deans have someone else gather the data, such as graduate assistants, administrative assistants, assistant or associate deans, or department heads, but a few deans were directly involved in the data gathering.

A second suggestion was to allow ample time for the data gathering, for preparation of the self-study and reports, and for communication of the process to faculty and students. Deans repeatedly stressed the need to allow at least six months for departments and faculty to prepare their sections of the report. As one dean remarked, "They think this is like a business or a company where all you have to do is list your assets and liabilities and arrive at the bottom line. There is no bottom line and all of the decisions are basically subjective and take time." Some deans thought they needed a greater role in developing the review process to ensure the relevancy of the reviews.

Finally, the deans recommend that the bulk of their work be turned over to someone else with a long institutional memory because deans just do not have time to devote to routine review activities. Such delegates should be trusted by the dean, respected by the faculty, and capable of delivering the necessary reports in a timely fashion. Deans delegated this work to assistant and associate deans, institutional researchers, influential faculty members, and occasionally administrative assistants.

The role of assistant and associate deans differs substantially from the dean's role, primarily in the type of work that is performed. Some typical functions performed by assistant and associate deans are gathering data, clarifying terms, answering questions, attending meetings, making institutional arrangements for consultants, and summarizing findings into the final report. The assistant and associate deans described the process as a massive task and said they had to devote 100 percent of their time to it. When program reviews occurred at the same time accreditation reviews were scheduled, the assistant and associate deans spent two years in a review cycle.

These deans attempt in their gatekeeping role to buffer the faculty from the workload. They are the action or project officers who must garner the resources to achieve the tasks with minimal disruption to the academic program. The assistant and associate deans we surveyed were generally not involved in the design of the process and simply reacted to a process already defined (Breier, 1985; 1986a). They frequently interpret the data and thus are able to modify the academic units' response to the review. They must balance the workload between faculty and themselves to ensure that faculty have an opportunity to participate without overburdening them. Assistant and associate deans sometimes regarded the review as a "wasted time and motion study" and a "dirty job but someone has to do it." In a well-designed program review, this cynicism will be minimized.

Recommendations from the assistant and associate deans involved the scheduling of reviews. All agreed they needed more time, particularly if they were responding to more than one review. They felt that the review team, whether outside consultants or an internal team of reviewers, should spend more time on campus and in the classroom. They expressed frustration that their institutional data simply could not tell the whole story about the academic programs; review teams needed exposure to faculty and students to grasp the nature of the instruction and the true quality of the programs. Finally, these deans said that not enough recognition was given to themselves or to faculty who participated in the review process. They felt that it was a full-time job which required more resources than were typically provided.

Directors of Programs. Sometimes colleges may be organized in such a manner that directors of programs are involved in the program review process. These directors are not department heads, generally do not have authority over resources or faculty, and usually report to either the dean of the college or the chief academic officer. When they are involved in a program review, they usually assume the role of an assistant or associate dean. That is, they are the primary action officer for the review.

Their role differs from assistant and associate deans in that they have little direct control over faculty and must rely on someone else to solicit faculty involvement. They must be skillful in maintaining good relations with the faculty and ensuring adequate responses to the faculty. They are likely to work alone on the review, to have less institutional support for data gathering and report preparation, and to feel a strong sense of ownership in the outcome of the review. Since they often feel that the review is their personal responsibility, they are not as critical of the process as the assistant and associate deans. They seem to regard it as their job and take pride in doing it well.

Since only a few reviews used program directors in this role, their recommendations are limited. In general, the directors wanted more time and more interaction with the review teams. They also suggested having a follow-up meeting after the final report to discuss the findings.

Governing Boards and Legislators

Members of governing boards and state legislatures are chosen or elected because they represent the constituents of the colleges and universities. More often than not they come from backgrounds other than education, but they typically find in the program review process the need for in-depth knowledge about higher education. Staff members and executive directors of state agencies are often specialists in higher education and help direct the involvement of the boards and legislators in program reviews.

The program review process affords basically the only opportunity for members of the public through their representatives on the boards and legislatures to become deeply involved in the programs, services, and personnel at their colleges and universities. Such an opportunity brings with it duties, responsibilities, and concerns that can be overwhelming to the unprepared participant. Recognizing that each state and institution presents a unique circumstance, we have found that certain points of the program review process are critical to governing boards and legislatures (Breier, 1985; 1986b). It is these common elements we wish to discuss.

The involvement of governing boards and state agencies in the program review process ranges from minimal to extensive. It all depends on the type of governing board, the approach of the program review, and the personalities involved. We will describe some of the ways in which governing boards, state agencies, and their staffs may be involved in the process.

First, involvement in the program review depends on the institution's approach to the process. As noted earlier in Chapter Two, the five approaches to program review offer a wide range of constituent, agency, and board involvement. The level and intensity of involvement depend on which approach is chosen and whether the review is formative or summative.

In the case of formative reviews, which are usually consultant, survey, or self-study oriented, board members may not even see the final report or be aware that a review took place. This is particularly true at large research universities with hundreds of programs and at small, private liberal arts colleges that grant their chief executive officers almost complete autonomy over the academic programs.

With summative reviews, board members are more likely to be involved in the review process, especially if the consultant or survey-oriented approaches are used. The more widespread the involvement of the legislature and its constituents in higher education, the more likely it is that the governing board members will be involved. In some instances the board may have initiated the process or endorsed it. Governing boards and state agencies are assisted by staff members who have functions similar to those of institutional support personnel discussed in Chapter Five. Since the relationship of state-level staff to the various institutions is unique, it is described in the following section.

State-Level Staff Functions. State agency or governing board staff consists of those who are employed either by a state department or commission of education, a coordinating board, or a consolidated governing board. The staff members for these agencies are often asked to design and implement program reviews for many different types of institutions and programs. Because of their positions, these staff members can be very influential during the course of a program review. With this in mind, the state-level staff member must be primarily concerned with ensuring that the process will treat each institution fairly. In some instances, the staff member encourages the institution to design a review process to meet its needs. In other cases, the staff member acts as an interpreter to assist institutions in implementing the state-designed review process.

In order for the program review process to work properly, there should be sufficient campus involvement. One of the functions of the state-level staff member is to help secure institutional support and involvement in the reviews. One method is to visit with the institution's representatives, usually the chief executive officer or the chief academic officer, in order to emphasize the purpose of the review and to stress that a well-informed public or board can become a strong advocate for higher education in the state. After the initial design and implementation phase, the staff member should visit periodically with the institution's representatives in order to review the process and gather insights into its effect on morale and productivity.

If the review process involves consultants, state-level staff, or board members, the staff member is responsible for scheduling the various program visits or reports and coordinating these schedules when several institutions are involved. The coordination of this phase requires a considerable amount of time and attention to detail and is essential to the effectiveness of a large-scale program review. Since everyone involved in the process feels that their time is valuable, the scheduling should minimize travel and avoid wasted time.

Kansas has used the statewide review system for seven years. Once the self-studies are completed and submitted to the Kansas Board of Regents, staff members read and synthesize all the reports and prepare them for presentation to the board members. The Board of Regents academic affairs officer and other staff play a key role in this phase because it is their responsibility to see that the board has all the information necessary to make informed decisions. One staff member reflected: "The staff has to help the board by drawing them a map to highlight the key points and suggest areas of increased focus of attention."

Once the board has reviewed the reports and made any site visits that may be required, the staff member may be asked to prepare a final report that presents the findings of the consultants along with recommendations the institution may be required to follow. In the case of the consultant's report, the staff member may only have to provide technical assistance in preparing the final report.

The final phase of the Kansas Board of Regents process is the negotiation stage. The state board staff member, with the approval of the Board of Regents, discusses each recommendation with the institution's representative (usually the CEO or the CAO) and tries to reach an agreement on what future direction the institution will take with regard to the recommendation. In some cases the recommendations have the force of law—as, for instance, in state regulations governing the licensing or certification of teachers, nurses, and architects. In other cases, it is a matter of common understanding as to what the outcome of the review will be and what action the institution will take to correct any deficiencies that are noted. In Kansas the program review process has done much to improve the quality of the academic programs (Kansas Board of Regents, 1984).

The negotiation stage can require a great deal of staff members' time and can be highly political. Staff members should negotiate only with the principal parties as indicated earlier and not allow the discussions to involve other institutional representatives such as deans, chairs, or faculty members who may have a vested interest in a particular program. Political ramifications are an inevitable part of the program review, and every staff member must be aware of this factor. Staff members should remain sensitive to what has been described as the "tension between the reviewing authority and the institution" and try to keep the institution informed of all developments that occur during the program review.

Moreover, staff at all levels must remember that institutions, both individually and collectively, can represent a powerful lobbying force within a state. Whenever a program or college feels threatened by an action that is contemplated by the reviewing authority, its constituents and supporters will rally to defend it. A good example of this response occurred in a midwestern state where the results of one program review led the state board to propose the elimination of all graduate programs at one institution. The institution sent letters to all its alumni and supporters asking them to contact their legislators regarding the proposed eliminations. Questions were raised as to whether certain meetings violated the state's open meeting law, and these issues discredited, to some extent, the program review. Ultimately the institution was allowed to keep some of its graduate programs and actually received increased funding for graduate programs the next year.

Evidence (Breier, 1986a) indicates that coordinating boards are more persistent in pressing for program terminations than governing boards. Governing boards generally do not feel comfortable telling a CEO to eliminate a program because they themselves hired that officer and feel a sense of respect for his or her judgment. This respect is one element of political influence that is difficult to measure but is nonetheless present in most reviews. A staff member noted: "If I could, I would try to totally do away with any political considerations, political being in the large sense of the legislature and the governor, because the political processes cause knee-jerk reactions, and it is almost impossible to be objective about things in the political environment."

One outcome of the review, if done properly, can be increased appropriations for higher education in the state. Interviews conducted with legislative staff, board executive officers, and administrators (Breier, 1986a) indicate that the appropriations were increased because the legislature and the public believed that the institutions were operating efficiently and that the program review served as an accountability measure ensuring the careful expenditure of public funds. Any savings gained as a result of program changes should accrue to the institutions involved. If institutions are not allowed to benefit from the program review, its credibility is threatened and the entire process can become a witch-hunt to eliminate programs rather than improve quality.

Board Members. Board members are expected to know that a review process is under way, to have general knowledge about the approach, and to act upon any recommendations emerging from the process. It is this last duty that appears to cause the most concern for board members. If a program review is undertaken, the anticipated result is that some action will be taken. Board members should be able to forecast the possibilities that might arise—such as demands for more resources or calls for termination—and should be prepared to make decisions regarding these recommendations. Failure to act on recommendations is the most critical concern of those involved in the process.

Board involvement in the program review process varies greatly and is therefore difficult to generalize. In most cases, board members leave the design and implementation of the process to state or campus staff members. Board members almost never gather data or choose consultants but again should be informed about these issues. In one midwestern state, board members did participate extensively in the program review by assisting in the design and implementation stages. As the process was implemented, board members visited each campus where programs were under review and met with the faculty, administration, and students before reaching a final decision regarding the evaluations. This extensive involvement was found to be too time-consuming for the lay board members, however, and in succeeding years the number of on-campus visits was reduced. We do not recommend extensive involvement of board members and mention this case as an example where such involvement was not successful.

In another state, though, board members only received a report of the final actions taken by the review committee. This is seen as a minimum degree of involvement and is necessary to maintain the integrity of the program review. At one private college in the south, the dean was the only person who ever saw the results of the program review. He reasoned that the president and governing board were too busy with "more important" issues to be concerned with the academic programs. The faculty, however, regarded the process as the dean's hatchet for chopping his enemies, "and the result was an inferior program review process not worth the efforts expended."

Governing board members should be knowledgeable about program review policies and should be kept informed of the process throughout the design and implementation stages. Members should follow the principles of good review described in Chapters Two and Three and ensure that the process has adequate representation from key groups both inside and outside the institution.

Members should review the self-studies and reports resulting from the reviews. The most important action they can take is to support the review's recommendations. This ensures the credibility of the process, but, more important, it also ensures that the institution will be improving the quality of its programs. Members should also expect that the process will initially disrupt some campuses and upset some faculty members. In state reviews, moreover, the administration may regard the process as an intrusion into its institutional autonomy. Some recommendations may also dictate politically unpopular choices such as merging programs, increasing appropriations, hiring or firing faculty, even terminating programs. If the program review is conducted in an honest and open manner with a variety of evaluative criteria, any unpopular decisions resulting from the review will be minimized.

Board members we interviewed had several concerns. Lay board members often wondered how much involvement they should have in decisions regarding academic programs. Members were frequently reluctant to review documents and evaluate technical aspects of academic programs about which they were not very knowledgeable—for example, the role of ethics in professional programs such as architecture and law, the amount of field experience appropriate for education students, and the type of research relevant for professors at teaching institutions. One solution is to ask the board or institutional staff to provide more information on accreditation standards, programs at similar institutions, and practices across the nation. One board member expressed his concern in this manner: "If we couldn't know something entirely or 100 percent, I was not sure whether we should be making this type of decision." Other board members feel quite confident in this role and believe it is their job to make recommendations about the operation of institutions. Another concern expressed by board members was the trouble they had in comparing institutions, since each one is unique. Kansas, Oklahoma, and Iowa compare institutions to those in other states. This approach relieves the board of some of the burdens of comparison by having a group of institutions with similar characteristics to serve as a benchmark.

By far the biggest worry for board members was making the tough decisions regarding programs. Decisions involving faculty, budgets, and program mergers or terminations always create some discord in the public, the institution, and the board. One member said: "Initially, I thought we could quantify these decisions but in reality it is a subjective viewpoint that must be made and there is a lack of information or mechanisms for qualifying those subjective viewpoints." The program review may not reach a bottom-line judgment about academic programs. It will provide answers to some questions, raise other questions, and evaluate the remaining questions, but ultimately someone must weigh the evidence and render a verdict. If the review process is sound, the evidence will point to the appropriate evaluation and board members will feel confident relying on that evidence to follow through with needed actions.

Legislators and the Governor's Office. Legislative involvement varies from state to state, but all states have appropriations committees or education committees whose task is to make recommendations regarding higher education funding in the state. These committees are often very powerful and may become interested in program reviews, especially if they are statewide reviews. In several states, program reviews were initiated because the legislature was pressuring the colleges and universities to be more accountable for the funds they received. The program reviews were a way of proving to the legislature that the institutions were operating efficiently.

With few exceptions, legislators almost never get involved in program reviews but do act as interested bystanders. One exception is in South Carolina, where statutes provide for legislative appeal of state board program review decisions. At least one program has been appealed since its adoption in 1978. In this instance, the South Carolina Commission on Higher Education recommended termination of several associate degree programs at the University of South Carolina–Columbia. The university appealed the decision to a committee of the state House of Representatives. The committee upheld the appeal by the university, which according to statute negated the commission's recommendation. Within eighteen months, however, the university voluntarily terminated the programs. Although they are infrequently applied, South Carolina is the only state with legislative statutes that allow for institutional appeal to the legislature. All state agencies are subject to legislative intervention if the legislature so desires (F. E. Kinard, Senior Associate Commissioner for Academic Affairs, South Carolina Commission on Higher Education, personal correspondence, February 1989).

Legislators are more typically concerned that the process affords equal treatment to all institutions, that ample opportunity for participation is provided to students, faculty, alumni, and the community, and that the results will produce a better education for all the taxpayers in the state. They are most concerned when the program review is conducted by outsiders (that is, consultants) who know nothing about the state, when the results are not implemented, and when the review deeply affects an institution in their district. Good communication with key legislators throughout a program review will help in promoting understanding, improving relations, and minimizing problems.

Virtually every governor has a staff member responsible for the education policy in his or her state. These staff members research questions related to education and advise the governor on education issues at the state and federal level. Generally they are politically attuned to the governor's views on education, have worked in political campaigns, have had experience in education, and are therefore chosen for their political skills and ability to represent the governor's views on education. Essentially the job of the staff member is to reduce controversy and resolve educational issues within the state in keeping with the governor's views. The influence of these staff members on the program review process varies from state to state but is usually nominal. Those conducting program reviews should, however, be aware of these key figures and keep them informed of the process and its outcomes.

Sometimes the governor's staff member works closely with key legislative committees such as the appropriations committee or the educational oversight committee. These committees have different names in different states but can be distinguished by their common functions. Some states have legislative staff members who serve as education advisers to the legislature. Such advisers often become involved in statewide program reviews by negotiating changes in the process and influencing legislation affecting higher education budgets.

Summary

Administrative involvement in the program review process is crucial. Administrators at all levels link the institution to the outside world and interpret the academic environment to the external constituents. Depending on their role in the program review and their administrative style, administrators may have an active part to play in the process. The involvement of governing boards and legislatures in the process varies greatly from state to state and depends on the type of program review. Board members and legislators may want to know why and how the review is being conducted and to act on information resulting from the review. The process is regarded as a means of establishing credibility and accountability to the public and is viewed quite positively by both board members and legislators. A well-designed and well-implemented review process will yield positive results for administrators and institutions.

7

Linking Program Reviews to Institutional Assessment, Accreditation, and Planning

❋❋❋❋❋

In the preceding chapters we have described the essential steps in developing, conducting, and evaluating a program review and discussed the various perspectives that stakeholders share regarding the outcomes of the review process. Here we consider the ways in which program reviews interact with other institutional processes, the relationships between program review, accreditation, assessment, and planning, and the future role of program review in higher education.

Program reviews do not occur in a vacuum. Regardless of the purpose of program review, political, social, and economic concerns will affect the outcomes of the process. The object of program reviews is not to eliminate these effects. By its very nature, the program review often heightens awareness of the review's outcomes. Thus it is necessary to remember that a successful program review depends on adherence to the guiding principles outlined in Chapter One:

• Fairness: All programs must be evaluated objectively if results are to be meaningful.
• Comprehensiveness: All aspects of all programs at all levels must be reviewed.
• Timeliness: All programs must be reviewed on a regular, predetermined basis.

- Communication: Throughout the entire process, people involved in the review and key figures in the institution must be kept fully informed of the review and its results.
- Objectivity: The design of the process and the selection of personnel must ensure as much objectivity as possible.
- Credibility: The process must be perceived as being fair and equitable to all programs.
- Utility: The results of the program review must be used in the planning and budgeting of the institution.

Program reviews are not the only institutional evaluation process. Almost all institutions today are also involved in accreditation and assessment procedures. Successful program reviews build on these institutional activities and share responsibility for developing an overall institutional plan for the future. The links between program review, accreditation, assessment, and planning are discussed in the following sections.

Accreditation

One of the most widely established evaluation processes on most campuses is that of accreditation by an outside agency. The accreditation process has for over seventy years served higher education well. Institutions have voluntarily joined one of the six regional accrediting bodies and fifty-eight specialized accrediting agencies in order to confirm the quality of their academic offerings.

There are similarities between the accreditation process and program review. First, both processes require some form of self-study, some type of on-site visit, some form of evaluation report, and, finally, some type of recommendations. In fact, these two processes could be carried out simultaneously if the timing and schedules could be coordinated. Second, both accreditation and program reviews frequently use the same type of data to measure institutional operations. While different accreditation agencies use different terminology and data sets, most of the data needed for accreditation purposes are also used in program review activities as illustrated in Table 10.

Table 10 indicates that the data needs of both accreditation and program review can be divided into descriptive and judgmental categories. Descriptive data include average salaries of faculty, student credit hours, and cost per student credit hour. As illustrated in Table 10, three of the categories are identical in program review and accreditation. In two categories, average salaries and cost per student credit hour, simple calculations can be done on data gathered in the program review to derive the necessary information for accreditation. In the judgmental category, all of the data listed are used in program review and can be inferred from data used for accreditation.

As institutions experience multiple evaluations from both accrediting agencies and program reviews, the collection and reporting of the data described in Table 10 become time-consuming and unmanageable. Efforts have therefore been initiated to develop a basic set of data to assess the current

Table 10. Comparison of Sample Program Review and Accreditation Data.

Category of Data	Used for Program Review?	Used for Accreditation?
Descriptive		
• Average salaries	Yes	Can be calculated
• Direct operating expenses	Yes	Yes
• Student credit hours	Yes	Yes
• Number of graduates	Yes	Yes
• Cost/student credit hour	Yes	Can be calculated
Judgmental		
• Adequacy of facilities	Yes	Inferred
• Adequacy of support staff	Yes	Inferred
• Adequacy of competitive salary	Yes	Inferred
• Assessment of leadership	Yes	Inferred
• Peer ratings	Yes	Inferred

state of an institution or program. In 1985 a joint project funded by the Ford Foundation for this purpose resulted in *A Common Language for Postsecondary Accreditation* (Christal and Jones, 1985), which presented a common set of data definitions used in accreditation activities. These definitions have not, however, been widely accepted by the accrediting agencies because each accrediting body prefers its own classifications. Continued efforts are needed to encourage accrediting agencies to adopt standard data elements and to incorporate them into program reviews. Since most program reviews are institutionally developed, the process can easily be adjusted to conform to accreditation definitions.

Several institutions and at least two states, Pennsylvania and Maryland, are considering combining their program reviews with accreditation visits. Such efforts can result in a considerable savings of time and resources, but several important differences between these two processes should be considered. The first concerns the purposes of the reviews. Accreditation studies are typically formative reviews aimed at program improvement and attempt to measure what has already occurred against some predetermined standards. Recently, regional accreditation agencies have begun to require outcome measures and comparison of what an institution *says* it is with what it is in practice. A program review, by contrast, depending on its purpose, may focus on program improvement or termination and may therefore be either formative or summative. A second difference between program review and accreditation studies is the issue of cost-effectiveness. Accreditation studies do not address this issue. Since most program reviews, particularly summative ones, do raise questions regarding a program's efficiency as well as its effectiveness, linking the program review with budgeting gives it a dimension beyond that of an accreditation visit.

Efforts to combine program reviews with accreditation processes have been seen in several areas. Representatives from the Council on Postsecondary Accreditation, a specialized accrediting body, an evaluation expert, and one of the authors held a symposium recently to find ways in which program review and accreditation could join efforts to reduce the burdens on institutions (Breier, 1988). A notable example of such cooperation has occurred in teacher education. Under a major redesign of the National Council for Accreditation of Teacher Education (NCATE) initiated in 1986, state departments of education can now apply to NCATE for program approval status. Once status has been granted, the NCATE review can satisfy the state department's review as well. As of September 1988, fourteen of the fifty state departments of education had been granted program approval status (Kunkel, 1988). For teacher education programs in those states, duplication of program reviews has been lessened and evaluation is now done with nationally recognized standards.

Assessment

Largely as a result of the accountability issue, institutions are now assessing student outcomes in a multitude of ways. Recent studies indicate that approximately two-thirds of the states and all six of the regional accrediting agencies are involved to some extent in institutional outcomes (Banta, 1989a). Assessment of student outcomes can be defined as "any activity from the simplest to the most complicated directed at reaching a judgment" (Manning, 1986). Assessment commonly refers to the evaluation activities colleges and universities undertake to assess their students' achievement.

Originally assessment began as a means of determining what students had learned from a common core of knowledge or whether students had gained certain competencies. These early efforts resulted in pilot programs in competency-based learning such as the one at Alverno College. While assessment efforts differ from program to program, campus to campus, and state to state, there has been, in recent years, a decided shift in the assessment movement from student outcomes to program outcomes (Cook, 1989, p. 2). This shift has created areas that, like accreditation studies, can be included as part of program review activities. For example, the University of Illinois at Urbana–Champaign has a multifaceted assessment approach that includes the Council of Program Evaluation

(COPE). The survey instrument is designed to measure students' opinions and satisfaction with various aspects of their departments. This information is compared with other departmental data such as the unit's administration, its national reputation, and historical data on tenure, promotion, courses, and budget. Units are reviewed on a cyclical basis (Gray, 1989). Such assessment efforts can easily be fit into the ongoing program reviews at any institution and can enhance both processes.

While there are standardized assessment instruments such as the ACT examinations, the College Outcome Measures Project (COMP), and, more recently, the Academic Profile and Educational Assessment Series (EAS), many institutions are developing their own instruments for measuring what a student has learned during the course of a college career. These individualized efforts give rise to more opportunities for sharing data between assessment and program review activities. Program assessments can be designed so that the information gathered during that process becomes one of the criteria for the program review.

An example of collaboration between assessment and program review is found at the University of Tennessee, Knoxville. Banta (1989b) reports that one of the humanities departments used assessment data in a self-study which then enabled the department to pinpoint the strengths, weaknesses, and future direction for the department. External reviewers confirmed the conclusions, and recommendations were made to further strengthen the department.

Assessment should be made as much a part of the program review as possible. But like accreditation, assessment has not been tied to planning and budgeting and therefore falls short of a review process in forming judgments about a program. In some states, such as Illinois and Ohio, assessment processes are being encouraged as part of program review and statewide planning. Such encouragement will assist in institutionalizing assessment and integrating it into ongoing processes. Community colleges, in particular, have had difficulty in conducting assessments due to limited resources and wide variations in students and programs. McIntyre (1989) notes that only if assessment is tied to institutional planning, review, and accreditation can community colleges hope to benefit from their efforts. A good starting point for integrating assessment data into the planning and budgeting process is to include them as a criterion for the program review. Thus student outcome data become one measure of program effectiveness, which in turn is one criterion in a program review's data set. As colleges and universities become more experienced in assessment, the natural integration of assessment and program review will occur.

Planning

The role of program review as a subprocess of strategic planning has been described as that aspect in which the internal strengths and weaknesses are assessed (Keller, 1983) and internal capabilities are determined (Caruthers and Lott, 1981), thus contributing to an overall assessment of an institution that leads to a strategic plan.

Program review, while useful in identifying academic strengths and weaknesses, makes numerous other contributions to a strategic planning process:

- Helps contribute to overall institutional quality
- Helps provide for institutional accountability (improved public relations)
- Helps determine institutional strengths and weaknesses
- Helps provide guidance for program improvement
- Helps assess the institution's competitive advantage
- Helps define the institution's mission
- Helps give faculty, administration, and board of trustees a sense of good stewardship
- Helps in budget allocation and reallocation
- Helps identify institutional priorities
- Helps contribute to the institution's overall effectiveness

In all of these ways, the program review can have a varied and complex relationship to an institution's strategic planning process. The specific impact of strategic planning on these dimensions may be positive or negative.

Since program review is a subprocess of planning, it is not surprising that the relation between the two, according to our survey responses, is primarily a one-way relationship. As we have just seen, program reviews can make several contributions to the planning effort, whereas planning contributes overall strategy guidance to the review process. Strategic planning provides the overall framework within which program review, as a tactical aspect of planning, is developed and implemented.

In examining the relationship between program review and strategic planning (including budgeting) in various institutions, four patterns can be identified: (1) no relationship, (2) linkage, (3) integrated, and (4) program review as a driving force. The first pattern shows no relationship between program review and planning. This pattern has the advantage of being purely formative. That is, the review is for the exclusive use of the participants for the purpose of program improvement; no one outside the unit uses the results for planning and budgeting. While this relationship (or nonrelationship) apparently exists in a few institutions, it is hard to believe there is no interaction between program review and the other management processes, since even self-improvement reviews are bound to produce requests for additional resources, which by their very nature establish a relationship with planning and budgeting. Nonetheless in a few institutions the relationship is so remote that the respondents claim it does not exist as a matter of institutional policy, management process, or tradition.

In the second pattern there appears to be linkage between program review and planning. Here planning, program review, and budgeting are related, though usually in informal ways. As one respondent explained: "The provost, who is responsible for the program reviews, also participates in the planning and budgeting process and will, on occasion, draw upon the reviews in making planning and budgeting decisions . . . usually with respect to those programs which stand out in the reviews as being exceptionally poor or exceptionally in need of additional resources." The linkage between program review and planning is generally less positive than in other patterns, primarily because of its inconsistent application, which is often viewed in such negative terms as "political," "showing favoritism," "subjective," and "punitive." The fact that it is applied only selectively (as the previous quote suggests) is perhaps the biggest liability of this pattern. The linkage pattern also appears to blur the purpose of the reviews, which is claimed to be program improvement. Concerns about a "hidden agenda" are frequently raised in many institutions having this pattern of relationship. Those who obtain additional resources are, of course, not as likely to raise questions as those whose programs have been hurt in the planning and budgeting processes. On the positive side, this approach allows a greater degree of flexibility for administrators. As one administrator noted: "The key administrators can use their own judgment and expertise in its use."

A third pattern is evidenced at institutions where program review is integrated with planning and budgeting. This pattern has the advantage of consistency between the review efforts for each program, and the purposes of the review are usually clearly known within the institution (or at least they ought to be). For whatever reasons, faculty appear to be more knowledgeable about planning, budgeting, and review in institutions using this approach. Because of the clear relationship to budgeting and planning, a program's financial aspects undergo greater scrutiny in the reviews. In institutions using this approach, the reviews are but one element of the planning and budgeting processes, along with other factors such as accreditation reports. The disadvantages of this approach include a tendency for the program's proponents to be less than candid in their appraisals because negative comments might be used to cut back the program or even eliminate it. This appears to be especially true where the program's faculty have primary responsibility for conducting the review, although the tendency to be less than candid is even reported where outside consultants have the primary recommending role. Similarly, there is also a slight tendency for the reviews to be overly positive (especially in the self-study materials prepared by the program faculty).

In the fourth pattern, the program review is a major driving force for the planning and budgeting process. Because of the pivotal role it plays in institutions having this pattern, the program review takes on much greater importance within the institution. Thus considerable stress may be associated with the reviews. Some think this is beneficial because "it forces attention on qualitative improvement," while others feel it distorts attention from program quality to "program review quality." As one respondent noted: "Quality reviews become synonymous with a quality program, and this can be pure foolishness." Even in institutions with this type of pattern, the program review is rarely the only piece of evidence considered in planning and budgeting (although the review is seldom ignored). The primary advantages of this pattern have been described as follows: "The basis of decision making is well known because the review reports are public information available for all to see" and "It reduces the subjectivity of the planning and budgeting process."

Regardless of the pattern that institutions follow with respect to program reviews, it is clear that the process will not remain static. As faculty and administrators change and as the institution's environment requires it, the process of program review will grow to fit the needs of the higher education community.

The Promise of Program Reviews

As colleges and universities move into the next decade, we see the program review becoming far more institutionalized than at present. The program review, along with assessment and accreditation, will become part of the routine institutional processes resulting in improved programs and greater effectiveness. These three processes are all part of strategic planning and represent different aspects of the overall evaluation. Faculty and departments will regard program reviews as much a part of everyday life as book orders. Administrators will use the results of program reviews as readily as they now study their enrollment data.

As colleges and universities begin to institutionalize the program review, they will become more efficient in reviewing programs, refining data collection, and streamlining the process. Institutions will find new ways to share data and will, in fact, collect data on students and programs at far more regular intervals. Using natural built-in data collection points, program reviews will occur on a continuous, not a five-year, cycle. Reports will be prepared in a matter of weeks, and administrators and faculty will know far more readily the status of their programs within an institution.

The program review, when done successfully, can lead to the improved efficiency and effectiveness of higher education. Coupled with an active strategic planning process, institutions can map their futures in ways that will ensure their continued growth and development. The challenge for higher education in the twenty-first century is to respond to its environment. The program review is one of the tools faculty and administrators can utilize in guaranteeing a successful response.

Summary

The program review is only one of the many activities that occur on college campuses every year. These activities are shaped and guided by other ongoing processes including accreditation studies, assessment, and planning and budgeting. Administrators will use the data collection and study phases of the accreditation and assessment efforts as part of their program review activities. Good communication between these activities is essential, therefore, and can be facilitated by centralizing these efforts in one office.

The contributions of the program review to planning and budgeting are numerous. Since the program review is a subprocess of strategic planning, it is important that it be successful. In previous chapters we have described the essential steps in developing, conducting, and evaluating a program review. If the principles suggested in this book are applied and evaluated, a successful program review will result.

References

Aldrich, H., and Herker, D. "Boundary Spanning Roles and Organizational Structure." *Academy Management Review,* 1977, *2,* 217–230.

Baker, E. L. "Tests and the Real World." In S. J. Hueftle (ed.), *The Utilization of Evaluation.* Proceedings of the Minnesota Evaluation Conference. Minneapolis: Minnesota Research and Evaluation Center, 1983.

Banta, T. "On the Crest of the Wave." *Assessment Update,* 1989a, *1* (1), 3.

Banta, T. "Weaving Assessment into the Fabric of Higher Education." *Assessment Update,* 1989b, *1* (2), 3.

Barak, R. J. "Program Reviews by Statewide Higher Education Agencies." In J. K. Folger (ed.), *Increasing the Public Accountability of Higher Education.* New Directions for Institutional Research, no. 16. San Francisco: Jossey-Bass, 1977.

Barak, R. J. *Program Review in Higher Education.* Boulder: National Center for Higher Education Management Systems, 1982a.

Barak, R. J. "A Perspective of the Antecedents, Present Status, and Future Developments of Academic Program Review in Higher Education." Paper presented at annual meeting of

129

the Association for the Study of Higher Education, San
Antonio, Texas, February 1982b.

Barak, R. J. "Role of Program Review in Strategic Planning." *Professional File,* no. 26. Tallahassee: Association
for Institutional Research, 1986.

Barak, R. J., and Berdahl, R. O. *State-Level Academic Program
Review for Higher Education.* Denver: Education Commission of the States, 1978.

Barak, R. J., and Miller, R. J. "Rating Undergraduate Program Review at the State Level." *Educational Record,* 1986,
57, 42–46.

Breier, B. "Program Review Policy in Intent, Implementation,
and Experience: A Case Study." Unpublished doctoral dis-
sertation, Department of Educational Administration and
Higher Education, University of Kansas, 1985.

Breier, B. *Case Study Program Review Activities at 5 Selected
Colleges and Universities.* Abilene: Hardin-Simmons University, 1986a.

Breier, B. *A Consultant's Perspective on Program Review Activities.* Abilene: Hardin-Simmons University, 1986b.

Breier, B. "Assessment Linkages: Program Review and Accreditation." Paper presented at annual meeting of the Association for the Study of Higher Education, St. Louis,
November 1988.

Brinkman, P. T. (ed.). *Conducting Interinstitutional Comparisons.* New Directions for Institutional Research, no. 53.
San Francisco: Jossey-Bass, 1987.

Caruthers, J. K., and Lott, G. B. *Mission Review: Foundation
for Strategic Planning.* Boulder: National Center for Higher
Education Management Systems, 1981.

Cheit, E. F. "What Price Accountability?" *Change,* 1975, 7,
28–34.

Chelimsky, E. "Improving the Cost Effectiveness of Evaluation." In M. C. Alkin and L. C. Solmon (eds.), *The Cost of
Evaluation.* Newbury Park, Calif.: Sage, 1983.

Christal, M. E., and Jones, D. P. *A Common Language for
Postsecondary Accreditation: Categories and Definitions for
Data Collection.* Boulder, Colo., and Washington, D.C.:

National Center for Higher Education Management Systems and Council for Postsecondary Accreditation, 1985.

Christal, M. E., and Wittstruck, J. R. "Sources of Comparative Data." In P. T. Brinkman (ed.), *Conducting Interinstitutional Comparisons.* San Francisco: Jossey-Bass, 1987.

Ciarlo, J. A. (ed.). *Utilizing Evaluation.* Newbury Park, Calif.: Sage, 1981.

Clark, M. J., Harnett, R. T., and Baird, L. L. *Assessing Dimensions of Quality in Doctoral Education: A Technical Report of a National Study in Three Fields.* Princeton, N.J.: Educational Testing Service, 1976.

Conrad, C. F., and Wilson, R. F. *Academic Program Reviews.* Higher Education Reports, no. 5. Washington, D.C.: ASHE-ERIC, 1985.

Cook, C. "FIPSE's Role in Assessment: Past, Present, and Future." *Assessment Update,* 1989, *1* (2), 2.

Craven, E. "Evaluating Program Performance." In P. Jedamus, M. Peterson, and Associates, *Improving Academic Performance.* San Francisco: Jossey-Bass, 1980.

Ewell, P. T. (ed.). *Assessing Educational Outcomes.* New Directions for Institutional Research, no. 47. San Francisco: Jossey-Bass, 1985.

Florida Postsecondary Education Planning Commission. *A Study of Postsecondary Education Accreditation.* Tallahassee: Florida Postsecondary Education Planning Commission, 1986.

Gardner, D. E. "Five Evaluation Frameworks." *Journal of Higher Education,* 1977, *48,* 571–593.

Gray, P. J. "Campus Profiles." *Assessment Newsletter,* 1989, *1* (2), 4.

Heydinger, R. B. "Does Our Institution Need Program Review?" Paper presented at 18th annual forum of the Association for Institutional Research, Houston, Texas, May 1978.

House, E. R. (ed.). *New Directions in Educational Evaluation.* Philadelphia: Palmer Press, 1986.

Joint Committee on Standards for Educational Evaluation. *Standards for Evaluations of Educational Programs, Projects and Materials.* New York: McGraw-Hill, 1981.

Kansas Board of Regents. "Program Review in the Regents System." Photocopied. Topeka: Kansas Board of Regents, 1984.

Keller, G. *Academic Strategy.* Baltimore: Johns Hopkins University Press, 1983.

Kells, H. R. *Self-Study Processes: A Guide for Postsecondary Institutions.* New York: Macmillan, 1983.

Kitto, H.D.F. *The Greeks.* Baltimore: Penguin Books, 1969.

Kuh, G. D., and Ransdell, G. A. "Evaluation by Discussion." *Journal of Higher Education,* 1980, *51,* 301–313.

Kunkel, R. "Assessment Linkages: Program Review and Accreditation." Paper presented at annual meeting of the Association for the Study of Higher Education, St. Louis, November 1988.

Light, R. J., and Pillemer, D. B. *Summing Up: The Science of Reviewing Research.* Cambridge: Harvard University Press, 1984.

Long, J. P., Minugh, C. J., and Gordon, R. A. *How to Phase Out a Program.* Special Publication Series, no. 42. Columbus, Ohio: National Center for Research in Vocational Education, 1983.

McIntyre, C. "Assessment in Community Colleges." *Assessment Update,* 1989, *1* (1), 13.

McLaughlin, J. A., and others (eds.). *Evaluation Utilization.* New Directions for Program Evaluation, no. 39. San Francisco: Jossey-Bass, 1988.

Madaus, G. F., Scriven, M., and Stufflebeam, D. L. (eds.). *Evaluation Models: Viewpoints on Educational and Human Services Evaluation.* Boston: Kluwer-Nijhoff, 1983.

Manning, T. E. "The Why, What and Who of Assessment: The Accrediting Association Perspective." Paper presented at 47th Invitational Conference, New York, 1986.

Melchiori, G. S. *Planning for Program Discontinuance.* Higher Education Reports, no. 15. Washington, D.C.: ASHE-ERIC, 1982.

Merwin, J. C. "Dimensions of Evaluation Impact." In S. J. Hueftle (ed.), *The Utilization of Evaluation.* Proceedings of the Minnesota Evaluation Center. Minneapolis: Minnesota Research and Evaluation Center, 1983.

Mims, H. S. "Program Review and Evaluation: Designing and Implementing the Review Process." Paper presented at 18th annual forum of the Association for Institutional Research, Houston, Texas, May 1978.

Nevo, D. "The Conceptualization of Educational Evaluation: An Analytical Review of the Literature." In E. House, *New Directions in Educational Evaluation.* Philadelphia: Palmer Press, 1986.

Patton, M. Q. "Integrating Evaluation into a Program for Increased Utility and Cost-Effectiveness." In J. A. McLaughlin and others (eds.), *Evaluation Utilization.* New Directions for Program Evaluation, no. 39. San Francisco: Jossey-Bass, 1988.

Popham, W. J. *Educational Evaluation.* Englewood Cliffs, N.J.: Prentice-Hall, 1975.

Ratzlaff, L. A. (ed.). *The Education Evaluator's Workbook.* Vol. 2. Alexandria, Va.: Education Research Group, 1986.

Rothman, J. *Using Research in Organizations: A Guide to Successful Application.* Newbury Park, Calif.: Sage, 1980.

Scriven, M., and Stufflebeam, D. L. *Evaluation Models.* Boston: Kluwer-Nijhoff, 1983.

Seigal, K., and Tucke, P. "The Utilization of Evaluation Research: A Case Analysis." *Evaluation Review,* 1985, *9* (3), 307–328.

Sharp, B. H. "Assessment Related Information from Institutional Data Systems." In J. O. Nichols, *Institutional Effectiveness and Outcomes Assessment Implementation on Campus: A Practitioner's Handbook.* New York: Agathon Press, 1988.

Smith, M. F. "Evaluation Utilization Revisited." In J. A. McLaughlin and others (eds.), *Evaluation Utilization.* New Directions for Program Evaluation, no. 39. San Francisco: Jossey-Bass, 1988.

Starr, H., and others. *Selecting, Analyzing, and Displaying Planning Information.* Columbus, Ohio: National Center for Research in Vocational Education, 1979.

Stevenson, J. F. "Assessing Evaluation Utilization in Human Service Agencies." In J. A. Ciarlo (ed.), *Utilizing Evaluation.* Newbury Park, Calif.: Sage, 1981.

Stufflebeam, D. L., and Shinkfield, J. J. *Systematic Evaluation.* Boston: Kluwer-Nijhoff, 1985.

Stufflebeam, D. L., and Webster, W. J. "An Analysis of Alternative Approaches to Evaluation." *Educational Evaluation and Policy Analysis,* 1980 (May–June), 5–19.

Trochim, W. (ed.). *Advances in Quasi-Experimental Design and Analysis.* New Directions in Program Evaluation, no. 31. San Francisco: Jossey-Bass, 1986.

U.S. General Accounting Office. *The Evaluation Synthesis.* Methods paper no. 1. Washington, D.C.: U.S. General Accounting Office, 1983.

Warmbrod, C. P., and Persavich, J. J. *Postsecondary Program Evaluation.* Columbus, Ohio: National Center for Research in Vocational Education, 1981.

Weiss, C. H., and Bucuvalas, M. J. *Social Science Research and Decision Making.* New York: Columbia University Press, 1977.

Wilson, R. F. "Assessing the Need for a Program Evaluation System." Paper presented at the conference on Planning and Conducting Program Evaluation and Review in Higher Education, St. Petersburg, Fla., January 1980.

Wilson, R. F. "Critical Issues in Program Evaluation." *Review of Higher Education,* Winter 1984, 7, 143–157.

Worthen, B. R., and Sanders, J. R. *Educational Evaluation: Alternative Approaches and Practical Guidelines.* White Plains, N.Y.: Longman, 1987.

Index